MW01092012

Mel Bay's
KLEZMER COLLECTION
For C Instruments

By Stacy Phillips

B♭ Version Available

Cover Credit: Jacqueline J. Galler

1 2 3 4 5 6 7 8 9 0

Visit us on the Web at http://www.melbay.com — E-mail us at email@melbay.com

I wish to thank the following without whose help this book would have been much the poorer.

Michael Koenigsberg and Dave Howard for access to their record libraries

Ida Marshall and Jonah Ehrenreich for translations and lyrics

Walter Zev Feldman and Andy Statman for the interviews

Walter Zev Feldman for information about recent research

Artie Rose at Acoustic Disc for the album

YIV0 (Yiddish Institute for Jewish Research) for access to their research materials

And especially Marlene "Cookie" Segelstein for help editing the music and Ellen Cohn for correcting the text.

INDEX

F. Freylakhs, Bulgars and Other Up-Tempo Tunes

G. Related Genres of Music:

Introduction

Klezmer, as a description of a musical genre, is a recent coinage. In Europe the appellation (though not the music) was sometimes regarded as a bit of an insult, intimating rough musicianship and lifestyle.

With the passing of the last generation of the people who lived the life that created this music, the meaning of the term, almost simultaneous with its introduction, became obscure. The expression has sometimes been incorrectly used to include Yiddish folk songs, theater music and work songs as well as experimental music fusions. Klezmer has nothing whatsoever to do with *Sunrise, Sunset!*

Here is my take on the subject. There is no argument that it is a condensation of two Hebrew words *klay* and *zemer* meaning "tools of music" ie. instruments. Klezmer is an instrumental form. It took on some of the style of the music of surrounding cultures in Central and Eastern Europe and continued to do the same in the United States. These influences include Russian, Ukrainian, Bessarabian, Romanian, and German folk musics as well as Western art and popular music. All this is leavened with a Middle Eastern sensibility derived partially from the music of the Ottoman Empire, but also from an unbroken stream of liturgical music stretching back to biblical times in Israel. Through all the assimilation klezmer was unmistakably a Jewish music, easily identified as such by people familiar with related genres.

It was originally connected with the certain rituals of Central and Eastern Europe Jewry, but definitely not synagogue music. During Klezmer's formative years the Turks had hegemony over much of Eastern and Central Europe. The Mid-Eastern style of the Jewish religious melody, specifically the cantillation of the *torah* and other biblical literature, did at least predispose Jews to Turkish influenced styles. Being text driven, these cantillations are often arrhythmic. Other "Oriental" influences are the absence (until relatively recently) of harmony and rarity of long "pure" tones. Instead notes are usually surrounded with graces, trills, chirps, crying effects, glissandi, etc.

Many of the Jews living in Russia, Ukraine, Bessarabia and Romania had emigrated from Germanic states between the Crusades and the end of the Middle Ages as a result of periodic spasms of that era's "ethnic cleansing". Many of the non-Eastern sounding tunes in the repertoire have their roots in German art and folk music. The lineage of the majority of Central and Eastern European "Ashkenazrc" Jews is controversial and an open academic question.

Their folk musics accompanied the Jews when a great wave of them emigrated to the United States in the late 19th-early 20th centuries. Klezmer was only one of the styles that interested these first generation Americans (mostly living in the area of New York City). There were Yiddish language folk songs, recordings of cantorial virtuosi and the music of the Yiddish theater (as well as American sounds). But none have enjoyed anything like the renaissance of klezmer music.

In the transfer from the first immigrants to the first generation born in America a great body of klezmer repertoire was lost. American-born Jews were already far removed from the culture that created the music. Andy Statman, one of the important musicians in the revival, says,"The music became just dance tunes. While they're great dance tunes, that's not what the music is all about". Read my interview with him for more.

In the late 1970's bands with young members began to form across America and attempted to recreate the sound of the old klezmer records. The how and why of the movement can be debated. Marc Slobin, one of the current academic experts on the subject, suggests that when Jews reached an "unconscious but critical level of acceptance" in the United States, klezmer was re-invented. Before that it was not a generally accepted "ethnic" symbol like Irish fiddling to another ethnic group or even Yiddish folk tunes.

Certainly the revival was affected by the then current interest in "ethnic" or "immigrant" roots. But there was something special about this particular type of music of the Yiddish world - its simultaneous alieness and familiarity, loopy energy, and emotional solo style that reached out from the old records and struck a resonance with a section of today's musicians.

Most of this music is usually associated with wedding celebrations and, in America, *bar mitzvahs*. My purpose is to present authoritative renditions of some of some of the best of that repertoire. I make no claims for this book as a scholarly work. I have probably used some jargon imprecisely without regard to academic definitions.

For an authoritative take on some of these subjects please read the interviews with Doctor Walter Zev Feldman and Andy Statman that follow the music.

The pronunciation of Yiddish varied greatly over the Yiddish speaking world, making transliteration unusually hopeless. Some lexicographers leave out vowels others find necessary. Then there is the problem of choice of vowels when included. I have tried to stay with one spelling except when it might cause problems finding the tune in question on an album.

I have usually used "kh" for the guttural clearing-the-throat sound associated with Yiddish. This is in response to the recent mauling of the older "ch" spelling by American television broadcasters who now pronounce that combination as in "cheese". (Try my favorite - "Yitzchak Shamir".) However, since it looked strange to me with "kh" in the specific case of the religious movement of the 18th century, I preferred "Chassid".

Titles are usually floating and not attached to a particular tune. Many of the melodies were named just to enable the record companies to put something on their labels.

I have chosen tunes that are both excellent examples of the klezmer's art and relatively easy to find on currently available recordings.

The transcriptions include a good portion of the embellishments which are so critical to authentic playing, while trying to avoid over-dense, unreadable notation. As is the case with all music, you cannot expect to learn its essence with the sole use of the written notation. Buy some of the records cited in the text to hear the very important details not included in the transcriptions, factors like: length and speed of glissandi, shifting dynamics over short time periods, the exact amount of legato versus staccato phrasing, mini rhythmic machinations, note entrances and exits etc. (See the discography for relevant addresses of record companies.) Experienced *klezmorim* (plural of "klezmer") may not even need the amount of detail I have chosen to include, and some will surely disagree with my selections. Hopefully there are enough particulars to help you appreciate and recognize the essence of a "klezmer" rendition of a tune when you hear it.

In some cases I combined pieces of different choruses or even different recordings to get a "best" representation of a piece. This is especially true of the ornamentation, which was constantly varied by the better practitioners of the art. Current sources for the music are listed in the short introductions to each piece. If no album name and record company is mentioned, it indicates that, to my knowledge, the tune is not commercially available as of the completion of this manuscript.

One obvious shortage in this book is the number of *doinas*. These important components of the klezmer repertoire are rubato or semi-rubato explorations of modes by a solo instrument accompanied by simple, repetitive obligattos. The lack of steady rhythm by soloist and (usually) accompaniment, along with dense embellishments, make a musically readable transcription a very difficult task indeed. I have included only two by way of introduction and placed them at the end of the first music chapter. My advice is to learn doinas by ear.

The klezmer portion of this book is divided into chapters of slowish tunes, horas and up-tempo pieces. Be aware that melodies can be played at various speeds and meters. Feel free to experiment with widely ranging tempos or even turning *freylakhs* and *khosidls* into *horas* and vice-versa.

Study them diligently, then enjoy the pleasure of making and listening to great music.

New Haven, Connecticut - November, 1995

Interpreting the Notation

"Interpret" is the key word. Do not be a slave to an exact reading of the music. In order to play these transcriptions intelligently and sympathetically, you should listen to accomplished practitioners of klezmer. Purchase some of the records cited in the accompanying texts and go to concerts featuring the new generation of klezmer musicians.

These transcriptions are not meant to be sight read. There is a bit too much detail to be accounted for to allow you to just "blow" through a piece.

Occasionally I have commented on the style of accompaniment. If not mentioned you can assume some sort of "oom-pah" style rhythmic back-up. (This does not include terkishes and horas whose rhythm is discussed separately in the text.)

****

Here is some commentary on the eccentricities of my notation.

WATCH OUT FOR NON-STANDARD KEY SIGNATURES!! Though these may slow you at first sight, they are a truer representation of the music than diatonic signatures with many accidentals. There are a number of situations where the Western concept of key signature is not applicable in an elegant manner, but again I attempted to minimize the number of accidentals

I have only noted slurs when I felt that a particular phrasing was essential for a specific figure. Eighth note triplets usually are not slurred while all faster ones and grace notes are.

This symbol is an instruction to repeat the previous measure:

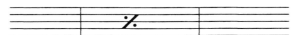

Notes are trilled up to the next note of the scale unless otherwise indicated. The older generation musicians varied their trills with each chorus. Some of the trills are "half-fingered" ie. the finger on the trilled note is not completely pressed down on the auxiliary note. This is typical of Gypsy and even some Irish and swing music.

a] Diagonal lines indicate short, quick slides up to or down from (depending on their direction) the specified note. When sliding up, the initial pitch is given no duration; when sliding down the same is true for the final pitch.

b] Jagged lines connecting two notes indicate a continuous glissando connecting them. Both notes have specified durations. When played with a bowed instrument, do not change bow direction during this move. With a wind instrument, play with one breath.

c]A curved arrow after a note symbolizes an exceedingly fast downward flick off the indicated pitch performed on the last instant of the duration of the note. On clarinet this gives a distinctive chirp-like effect. On a violin it sounds a bit more crying-related.

d]A vertical arrow above a note indicates that the note is played a bit sharp. This is used in slide maneuvers.

The duration of a grace note is taken from the previous note unless otherwise indicated in the introduction to a tune.

There is a typical motive that is meant to sound like an emotional catch in the throat or sob. The literal phrasing has been notated with various durations:

The usual contour is "first note of motive up one (occasionally two) scale steps, then down to the scale step beneath the first note" as in:

The second note is often only partially fingered to give a touch of pitch but effecting a definite vocal-like "catch" between the first and third notes. A parentheses around the second note indicates this technique. This "sob effect" is usually mentioned in the introductions to the entries that use them.

Infrequently this motive crosses bar lines. It is always phrased legato, eg. with one bow on violin or a continuous breath on a wind instrument.

When I asked Andy Statman about it he said that there are different ways of phrasing and articulating this motif. It depends on the tune and where in the tune it is being played.

I have occasionally notated the typical ending for up-tempo tunes, a chromatic run from the fifth note of the scale up to the tonic. From the several examples given you should be able to apply it to any tune. The position of the endings of most of the old recordings were dictated by the length limitations of old 78's, not by the "composition" of the piece.

A parentheses around an accidental is either a courtesy symbol (to remind you of the original key signature) or a signal that the natural pitch is an alternate way to pitch a note or that the original recording was unclear.

The capital letters above the staff are chordal accompaniment. There is no one correct way to accompany this music. Harmony is a relatively recent addition to klezmer music, only becoming typical in the 20th Century. Feel free to use these as a starting point for your own interpretations. Occasionally I have included an alternative in parentheses.

When there is a particularly interesting bass line I have notated it in capital letters beneath a diagonal line under the chord. If the chord does not change during the bass line I usually left out the chord identification and just noted the bass. For example:

An alternate version of a particular section is marked with a prime, eg. section 3 and 3'.

When faced with a relatively quick burst of notes (eg. a string of 1/32 notes or 1/16 in a tune with otherwise almost all 1/4's and 1/8's) do not try to read the timing literally. These short passages are usually quick "smears" of sound. Squeeze the notes into the duration of the phrase without much regard to the individual notes. For example, see measure 8 of "Kallarash" in the "Hora" chapter.

A transcriber always has to face the problem of readability versus precision of music notation. The only way to really learn these tunes is to listen to the recordings. When first dealing with a new piece leave out the ornamentation to get a grasp of the basic tune. Sixteenth note triplets can be simplified by only playing the first note of the triplet for the entire eighth note duration. After this sort of "basic" rendition is under control begin to add trills, "sobs", graces, slides, etc.

"WALKING TUNES, KHOSID'LS, TERKISHES, AND OTHER SLOW-ISH TUNES"

This chapter consists of slow-ish tunes in 2/4 and 4/4 meters. There are several murky categories: khosidls, wedding marches and "seating tunes", Chassidic nigunim, and terkeshes whose performance style sometimes is hard to distinguish from a freylakh. I have included a sort of musical outline of two doinas representative of that part of the repertoire.

BAYM REBIN'S SUDE

At the Rabbi's Banquet is based on Abe Schwartz's 1917 recording ("Master of Klezmer Music - Volume One" Global Village 126 and "Klezmer Music" Folklyric 9034). This tune also can be found on The Klezmorim's "Streets of Gold" (Arhoolie 3011). It is played at a supremely unhurried pace, and filled with Old World atmosphere.

I have notated only some of the dense ornamentation of Schwartz's clarinet player Naftule Brandwein (sometimes spelled "Brandtwein"). The chirps connected to quarter notes as in measures 5 and 6 should be placed at the very end of the duration of each note. On the recording it sounds as if the 1/16 note runs in section 3 are slurred and glissed into a soupy gruel of pitch.

That's a G♯ in the key signature!

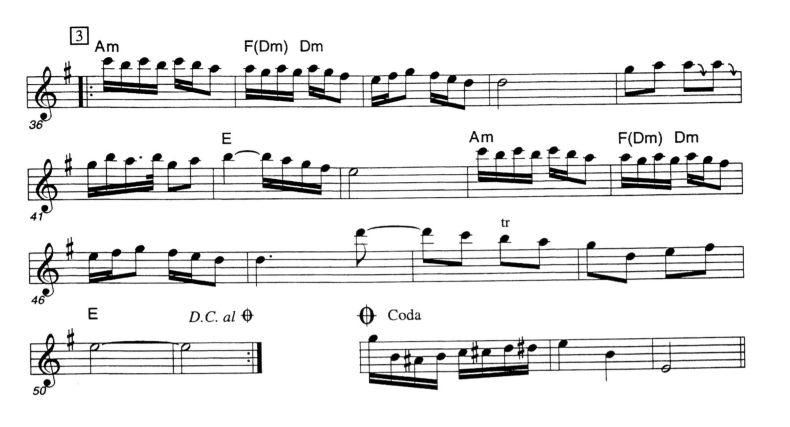

BERDICHIEVER KHOSID

This arrangement is based on the 1916 recording by the anonymous "Jewish Orchestra" that featured trumpet.

This section 3 is similar to section 2 of "Fon der Khope #2" found in the chapter of freylakhs.

A GLEZELE VAYN

A Glass of Wine is adapted from a recent recording by the Klezmatics ("Shvaygn = Toyt" - no label). There are some beautiful mode changes in the second and third sections. Watch the key signature in the second section!

EXCERPT FROM "TAKSIM"

Jacob Gegna recorded a taksim followed by this piece ca. 1917. (A taksim usually refers to the Turco-Arab manner of a rubato exploration of West Asian modes. It means something related to this, but different when referred to as the precursor of the Romanian doina.) Despite the title, Gegna's performance seems to be a doina, although with perhaps less accompaniment then usual. The rhythmic non-doina portion of this recording that I have transcribed features Gegna's virtuosic violin with minimal assistance from a pianist. There is some variation in the notated metronome marking, as the musicians treat the tempo conversationally, peppering their performance with speech-like hesitations. For example in measure 20, they suspend the rhythm for just a moment as they hang on the G eighth note.

The "pizz." and "arco" markings in section 1 refer to plucking then bowing respectively. Measures 6 and 7 feature the typical klezmer "catch-in-the-throat" sob. The parenthetical notes are the upper end of the sob, only partially fingered, so more "felt" then sounded.

Gegna keeps his open G string droning through most of the third section. (Good luck to any clarinet players who attempt this.) The parenthetical D7 chord should only be played during the repeats.

The 1/32 note triplets in section 4 might be interpreted as two grace note plus a 1/16 (as in measure 27) or even two 1/32 notes and a 1/16 (as in measure 1). The difference between the measures 18 and 24 is the timing of the slide. The former is a bit slower and begins a bit earlier in the duration of the A note. The latter is very fast and sharply executed with quick release of the finger resulting in a klezmer "chirp".

The coda is played during the repeat of section 1. And follow the bouncing key signatures.

FREYLAKHS FUN DER KHUPE

This rollicking wedding march translates as *Freylakh from the Wedding Canopy*. (*Freylakh* refers to either a dance or, literally, *joy*.) Trills, quick triplets and wicked chirps help establish the mood. The rhythm of measures 14-15 shade into one another, and they can be played as written or both with the durations of 14 or 15.

Section 3 is a bit sedate compared to the first two. Simply remove a jot of swagger from your playing. The opening measures have tricky rhythm. The staccato quarter note and the 1/32 notes should be held about the same amount. As long as you manage to leave a small bit of breathing space at the indicated points, the desired effect will be achieved. You need not worry about playing it exactly as written.

This can be heard by Elenkrig's Orchestra on "Klezmer Music" (Global Village 104 and Folkways 34021) and by Andy Statman with Zev Feldman on Shanachie #21002.

Notice that the key signature in sections 1 and 2, using a C tonic, is used in other tunes in this book with either a D tonic eg. *Berdichiever Khosid* above, or a G tonic as in *Khasene March #2* later in this chapter.

GOLDEN WEDDING ANNIVERSARY

This arrangement of *Golden Wedding Anniversary* can be found on "Andy Statman Orchestra" (Shanachie 21004). It involves an exciting series of scale changes while F remains the tonic note. Watch out for the key signature in section three and four.

Statman trills a high F note during the entire third section.

The notated chord progression is only one of many cool possibilities. As opposed to *Freylakhs fun der Khupe* this Statman rendition is well-mannered and has a proper mien, performed with reserve.

GRICHESHER TANTZ

Greek Dance is based on the 1929 accordion solo in terkishe rhythm by Mishka Tsiganoff ("Klezmer Pioneers" - Rounder 1089). (What has been referred to as terkishe rhythm is the same as the Greek *sirto* dance rhythm.) There was a strong connection between Jew and Greek since the Hellenic Age, which continued through Turkish Ottoman rule. A shared repertoire existed especially in the Greek areas of Asia Minor.

The figures in the first ending of section 1 and the second ending of section 2 are the basic rhythm patterns of Tsiganoff's left hand.

KALEH BAZETSEN TERKISHE

This terkishe from the medley, *The Bride Is Seated* can be heard on "Andy Statman Orchestra" (Shanachie 21004).

KHASENE MARCH 2

Wedding Dance #2 is taken from the playing of violinist Leon Schwartz ("Leon Schwartz - Like a Different World" Global Village 109). It does not have as heavy an Eastern touch as most of the klezmer music in this book. Instead there is the obvious dominant-tonic harmonic movement of Western art music.

KHOSIDL #1

This piece was originally recorded by Belf's Orchestra in Romania in 1910 ("Klezmer Music" - Folklyric 9034). It represents the old country style of klezmer with no added Americanisms. The rhythm supplied by the horns backing up the lead clarinet is:

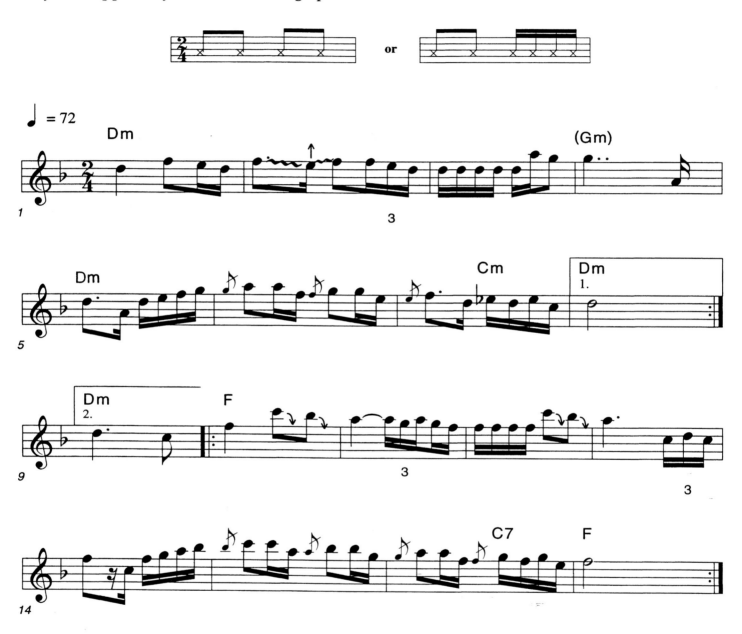

KHOSIDL #2

I learned this march-like piece from Andy Statman.   Watch out for the surprise change to C major in section 3.

"DIE KHASIDIM FORREN TSUM REBBIN"

This liturgical-type melody is part of a skit on the 1924 record of *The Chassids Visit the Rabbi* by Kandel's Orchestra ("Klezmer Pioneers" - Rounder 1089). It is played by violin an octave higher than notated here. There are lots of long, fast slides that I have not transcribed where the fiddler switches hand positions.

KHUSIDLEKH

This is one of the tunes on the Chassidic style medley on "Leon Schwartz - Like a Different World" (Global Village 109). The title is a plural form of "khosidl". Schwartz played it on violin with the accompaniment of seconding (chording) violin and bass.

KHSIDISHE NIGUNIM

This medley of *Chassidic Tunes* was recorded by the Boibriker (also spelled "Boyberiker") Kapele in 1927 ("Klezmer Music" - Folklyric 9034). The key may actually be E♭. Many of the fast triplets can be treated as trills.

In the first tune, the modulation from F major and D minor to D major in section 3 is especially effective. Violins take the lead on this piece and they pepper their note entrances with slides of varying speed and distance. These, along with the "sobbing"-like figures of a pair of 1/32 notes

(continued on page 27)

followed by 1/16's as illustrated below, make for an emotion filled piece. Only partially finger the upper pitch of the 1/32 pair to imitate a "catch" in the throat.

The second tune is filled with high spirits, partially induced by a brawny back beat supplied by the accompanists.

#2

KHUPAH TANZ #1

This *Wedding Dance #1* is another piece I learned from Andy Statman when he was a member of "Derekh Olam" ("Way of the World"), a klezmer *cum* old time southern music group.

Play the melody with a light attack, so that the wedding party dances on their toes, and does not trudge.

The Am-E7-A7 progression in section 3 is one of my all time favorites. Watch the G♯ key signature.

KHUPAH TANZ #2

The march-like *Wedding Dance #2* comes from a recording by Abe Schwartz ("Master of Klezmer Music - Volume One" Global Village 126). As usual, the trumpet plays as written and the clarinet plays an octave above. The accompaniment becomes more energetic for section 2 and I have notated the percussion accents.

29

KISHNIEV #1

This stately terkishe, named for a town that probably no longer exists, is based on the stylings of Dave Tarras ("Music for the Traditional Jewish Wedding" - Balkan Arts Center US 1002). When you play the series of consecutive G or A notes, phrase them legato but attack each firmly.

In the second half of the medley Tarras leaps into a freylakh that is transcribed in that chapter under *Kishniev #2*. He then plays *Kishniev #1* in freylakh rhythm. It's allowed. I read about it once in the talmud.

MAZEL TOV MEKHATONIM

This bouncy walking tune, *Good Luck to the In-Laws* is based on the 1919 version by the Abe Schwartz Orchestra on "Jakie Jazz 'em Up" (Global Village 101). The grace notes in measure 5 begin <u>on</u> the down beat.

The clarinet plays an octave higher than notated and occasionally peppers the first four measures of sections 1 and 2 with sustained or 'chirped' high G notes.

NIGUN

This rendition of the simply titled *Tune* is a Chassidic melody of the type now often played or hummed for long periods to induce the proper frame of mind for prayer. This class of instrumental music is properly not "true" klezmer music but it is so close that anyone familiar with klezmer would know how to get the right feeling. Andy Statman performed this piece on mandolin on his album "Klezmer Suite" (Shanachie 92005). Besides his great clarinet playing (he was a disciple of Dave Tarras) Andy is one of the foremost mandolinists in the world.

This version is a simplification of Statman's playing, omitting his many double stops, tremolos, trill, dynamics, and variations. The accompanists play a tango-like rhythm.

ORIENTALISCHE MELODY

This slow, mournful tune is based on the playing of violinist Max Liebowitz's recording from the early twentieth century. It sounds as if it is based on a liturgical melody. Liebowitz played it an octave higher than notated here.

A cymbalom echoes the melody, in the style of the Near East, with chords only faintly suggested.

OPSHPIEL FAR DI MEKHATONIM

Dave Tarras performed this medley on "Music for the Traditional Jewish Wedding" (Balkan Arts Center US 1002). The title translates roughly as *Prelude* (or *Overture*) *for the In-Laws*. For ease of reading I decided to notate the first in cut time. In terms of 2/4 meter (to compare it to the second tune) the first tune has a tempo of 60 beats per second.

The basic rhythm patterns on the first piece are:

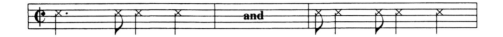

In measure 4 it sounds as if Tarras did not completely finger the 1/16 note C, resulting in a ghosted, glottal-like tone with only a suggestion of pitch.

The second piece is on the cusp between a khosidl and an up-tempo freylakh. It is possible that both tunes were played in the key of F.

#1

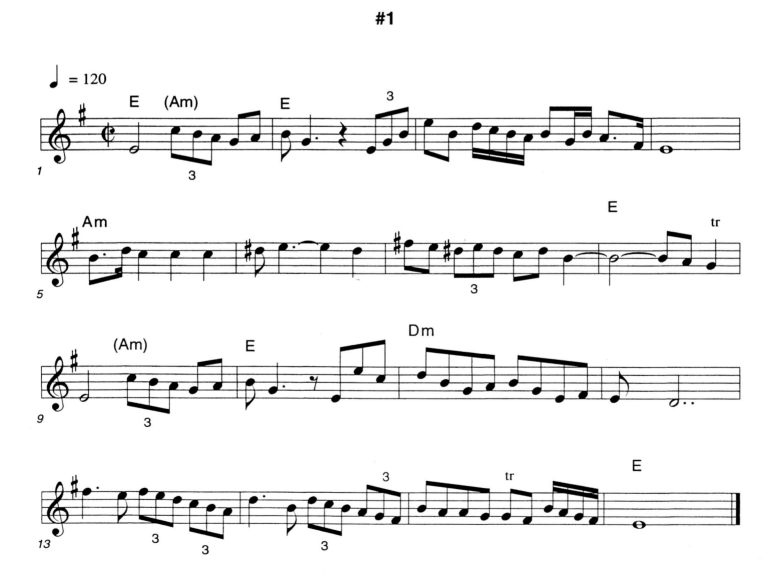

#2

DER REBBE IS GEGANGEN

This version of *The Rabbi Has Gone* is based on a version by Elenkrig's Orchestra ("Klezmer Music" - Global Village 104 and Folkways 34021). The first and third measures may be played:

Sections 3 and 4 have been transcribed an octave lower than played on the lead clarinet on the record, to keep the music within the range of most instruments.

The note durations of measures 35-36 and 39-40 shade into 1/4 note triplets. Take your choice.

DEM REBEN KHUSID

The Rabbi's Disciple was played at freylakh tempo in 1923 by my favorite klezmer clarinet player, the wild man from Galicia, Naftule Brandwein ("Jakie Jazz 'em Up" Global Village 101). His combination of technical control and fiery improvisation is unmatched on klezmer recordings. He plays this an octave higher than notated and fills his interpretation with many artful variations with each repetition. This piece may have been performed in the key of D minor.

Note the meter on this piece, chosen for ease of reading. The staccato-ed eighth notes in sections 1 and 3 are a subtle but distinct effect Brandwein employs each time this section is repeated.

In measure 17 he alternates a three beat B note with the chirped rendition I transcribed. Measures 27-28 are sometimes phrased as four consecutive B half-notes.

Khusid sometimes denotes a student or disciple instead of, literally, a Chassid.

DEM REBEN'S TANZ

I believe that this khosidl sounds best in as high an octave as is comfortable. In addition, the last four measures of section 2 might be played an octave higher relative to the rest of the transcription.

This rendition of *The Rabbi's Dance* is based on a 1929 recording by the Art Schryer Orchestra, currently available on "Klezmer Pioneers" (Rounder 1089).

RUSHISHE SHER #1

This piece is not played at the usual freylakh tempo of shers; it sounds more like a wedding march. The dissonant flatted fifth intervals of measures 3 and 11 stand out, as does the slick key change into section 3. I have heard bands alter the F sharp to F natural in measures 3 and 11, but that seems enervated to me. The descending bass line in section 2 is a fine contrast to the melody at that point.

Recordings of this piece can be found by I. J. Hochman's Orchestra on "Klezmer Music" (Global Village 104 and Folkways 34021) and by Andy Statman and Zev Feldman on their Shanachie album (#21002). On the latter this melody is called "Old Sher".

41

SIMKHAS TORAH

This ca. 1916 recording by Yiddesher Orchestra is named for the holiday that marks the ending of the annual cycle of reading the torah. (*Simkhas* is a Hebrew word with the connotation of "a happy occasion".) While the scale remains almost constant there are some charming chord changes marking the modulation between C minor and its relative major, E♭.

TANZ FAR ALLE MEKHATONIM

This tune is almost sufficiently lively to be a freylakh but I'll label it a khosidl on a split decision. The Abe Schwartz Orchestra recording upon which this is based sounds like a brisk march. The clarinet and violin soar an octave above this transcription while the trumpet plays as notated. The clarinet is responsible for most of the ornaments. The title translates as *Dance for All the In-Laws*. (*Mekhatonim* is the relationship between the two sets of in-laws, a concept with no comparative term in English.)

The slides in measures 9 and 15 begin immediately. The parentheses around the pitch indicate that you should not stay on that pitch, but begin slowly descending.

The grace notes in part 3 are <u>on</u> the downbeats.

43

DER SKYLINER KHOSID

Der Skyliner Khosid (a.k.a. *Sadegurer Khosid'l*) is based on recordings by the Andy Statman Orchestra ("Klezmer Suite" - Shanachie 92005) and the Abe Schwartz Orchestra ("Master of Klezmer Music - Volume One" - Global Village 126). The faster tempo marking is played by the latter.

You need not try to phrase the 1/32 figures exactly. Think of them as a smear of notes and jam them into their total duration willy-nilly. Andy Statman sometimes plays measures 21-22 as:

Play either section 3 or 3' (not both) with each repetition of the whole form. The predominant rhythmic figure is:

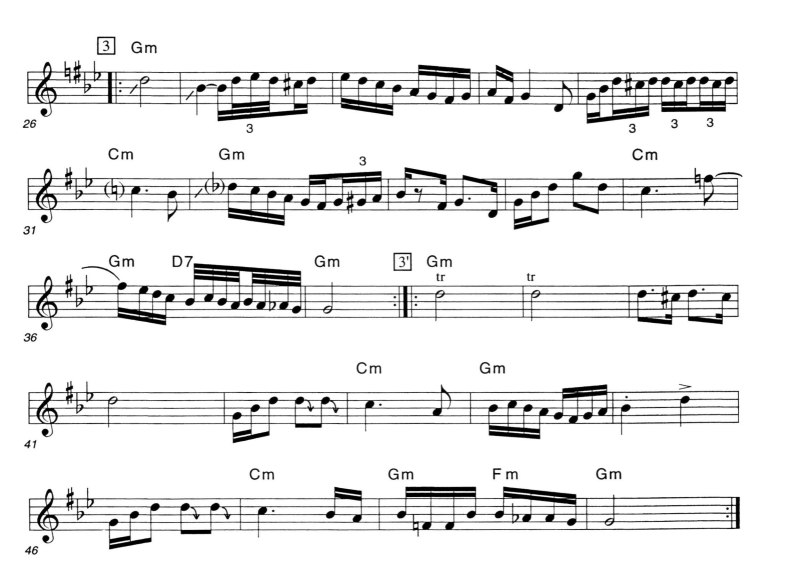

TERKISHE MELODY FROM "DOINA" MEDLEY #1

This is the first tune of a medley by S.Kosch ("Klezmer Music" - Global Village 104 and Folkways 34021). It exhibits the typical *terkishe* (actually Greek *sirto*) back up rhythm, albeit at a slow pace.

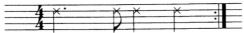

This ancient recording features florid flute and cymbalom accompaniment.

TISH NIGUN

This slightly kitsch-ey number has a very "bar mitzvah party" ambience. I am especially drawn to the Hollywood/Arab sound of the G minor to E♭ dominant chord progression. The is sounds cool against the terkishe *cum* tango of the percussion.

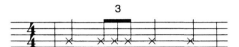

I learned it from a recording by Klezmer Plus, a band from New York City.

TERKISHER YALE VE-YOVE

This quick terkishe is vehicle for the great "old country" feel of Naftule Brandwein's clarinet recorded in 1923 ("Klezmer Music" - Folklyric 9034). The title refers to a Hebrew prayer, possibly the source of the basic melody. He explores three D scales, shifting with each new section.

You have to hear Brandwein's playing to appreciate my dense notation and his constantly shifting melodic rhythms. The durations transcribed here can only approximate his mastery of musical expression. That's a G♯ in the key signature.

He plays this an octave up. The dotted 1/8-1/16 phrases (eg. in measures 2 and 6) are swung a bit but the exact phrasing changes with each repetition. In the first measure of part 4, the grace note takes its time from the following G. Brandwein also plays that measure as:

The accompaniment basically plays the 1 and 5 notes of the chords through the entire piece.

This rhythm is the same as the Greek *sirto* and suggests connections between the Jews of Eastern Europe and the Greek inhabitants of the Turkish Empire of the 18th and 19th centuries.

49

TSIGANESHTI

This beautifully conceived piece is based on the clarinet of Dave Tarras ("Music for the Traditional Jewish Wedding" - Balkan Arts Center US 1002). The title refers to "gypsy-ness". Tarras's playing is always stately and under full control. Check out the seemingly constant and seamless flow from one mode to another. His phrasing in measure 5 is quite swing-y and behind the beat. My notation is a rough approximation.

With each measure Tarras phrases with differing levels of sputtering tounging, slurring, sliding, mini-dynamic swings, as well as variations of melodic pitches and rhythm. His artistry is at its maximum here, making the complexity seem simple. Digest all the subtleties of this performance and you will know a lot about klezmer music, even though it is based on a gypsy theme.

Tarras is accompanied by accordion and drums. The basic drum pattern is:

YIDDISH KHOSIDL

This entry is based on Max Liebowitz's violin playing. The parenthetical notes represent the partially fingered part of the "sob effect" that is explained in "Interpreting the Notation". There was sufficient variation in the repeat of section 1 to warrant it to be written out instead of using a repeat sign.

On the recording the piano plays measures 31 and 33 alone, with no rhythmic accompaniment. Following these rhythm stops, the next four measures are a joyous climax to section 3.

At the beginning of measure 4 the piano plays an E minor chord but D seems preferable to my ears. The 1st note of section 4 might be an E.

BA DEM ZEIDEN'S TISH

The march-like *At Grandfather's Table* is based on Dave Tarras's playing on "Music for the Traditional Jewish Wedding" (Balkan Arts Center US 1002).

In measure 29 the grace notes take their time from the previous note.

DOINA #1

This 1905 cornet solo by Mihal Viteazul is one of the few of the first generation of European (Romania) records also to be released in the United States. Because of its rubato phrasing and (usually the) absence of steady rhythmic pulse by accompanists, it is impossible to design accurate and precise transcriptions of doina using standard notation. However, since it is one of the staples of the recorded output of klezmorim I wished to have a couple in this book. There is no way to follow this musical outline without either having the recording or being very familiar with the doina style.

I chose this particular example for a few reasons. It is relatively lacking in dense embellishments that most of the old doina soloists seemed to revel in. They are the same kind of embellishments as in the rest of this book, but the rubato phrasing makes their notational interpretation chancey and subjective. In addition, this is one of the earliest recordings of a klezmer musician and it was made in Romania, reportedly the birthplace of the doina. Hopefully it represents a relatively early, "pure" and uncluttered approach. Finally it is easy to hear, having been re-released on "Klezmer Pioneers" - (Rounder 1089).

The accompaniment consists of a few other horns pedalling on the notes of the chords. Mister Viteazul leaves pauses of 3-7 seconds between motives (which I have labelled as if they were separate section). These separations are marked by dotted bar lines. Otherwise I have not employed measures because of the lack of meter. During these rests a lower pitched brass (a baritone horn?) plays:

The phrasing in the entire selection is very legato. Accidentals apply up to the next dotted line (except for the Bb in the key signature). My choice of beaming hopefully reflects Viteazul's phrasing.

Play the second motive three times at an accelerating tempo before pausing. The bracketed phrase in section 3 is played five times and sped up. In 3' the same phrase is repeated only four times, followed by a slowing down.

My interpretation of some phrases to be triplets is subjective. The timing seems to shift gradually between duple and triplet division of phrases. Then again, it could be my over-heated imagination.

After a final pause the entire band launches into an energetic freylakh.

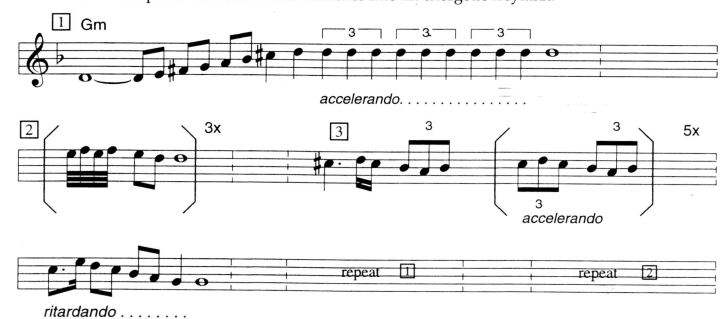

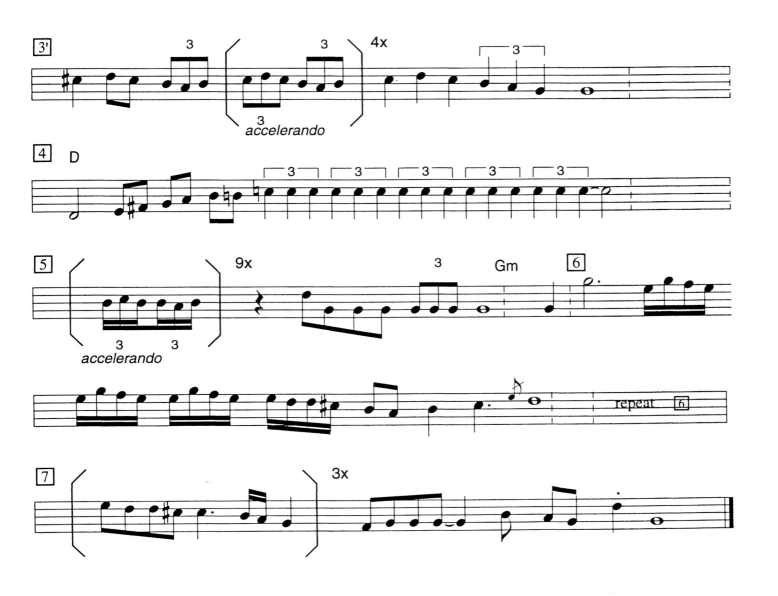

DOINA #2

Dave Tarras began his recording career in America in 1924. He was born into a family of klezmorim and raised in southeastern Ukraine. His clarinet artistry set the standard for fifty years. This entry was recorded in 1979 ("Dave Tarras - Music for the Traditional Jewish Wedding" - Balkan Arts Center 102) and can be used to compare the melodic approach to a doina by two Old World klezmorim, separated by 75 years. To comprehend the rhythmic aspect there is no substitute for buying the records.

In this arrangement an accordion supplies an arrhythmic chordal drone. I am using a subjective pulse in the *allegro* range (MM=104-120). The notation of various three note riffs as either 1/8 note triplets, 1/4 notes or 1/4 note triplets is subjective.

Refer to the introduction to *Doina #1* for an explanation of the symbols unique to these two selections.

Tarras' pauses between motives are no more than three seconds, and usually less. The parenthetical notes are part of the "sob-effect" discussed in "Interpreting the Notation".

To begin motive 2 there is a diminution of note duration during the opening B♭ minor arpeggio. The notes gradually shorten from something like a 1/4 to something like a 1/16.

In motives 3, 5 and 7 Tarras arranges the phrasing such that the accent marks where the motive begins and is a gentle accent. (Is this an oxymoron?) The previous notes can be considered a pick-up.

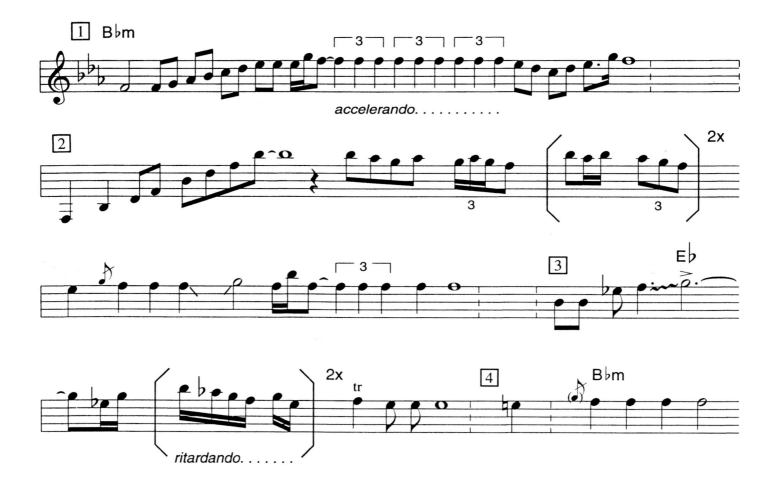

"HORAS"

"Horas" in klezmer music bear no resemblance to the tourist-y horas of modern Israel. (The duplication of names probably is caused by the historical intermingling of languages and peoples in Eastern and Central Europe) The horas in this book derive from a traditional dance from the Moldavia area of Romania and Ukraine. I have usually seen it written in 3/8 meter but I find it easier to read as 3/4. (Thereby all the note durations are doubled but the same relationships remain in the notation.) However <u>do not</u> treat these tunes as waltzes.

The backup rhythm is distinguished by playing on the first and third beats, omitting the second - making for a lurching, limping gait. For example, over Cm chords the bass instrument might play.

A typical variant could be

Their slow, portentous feel makes them fertile grounds for an overabundance of musical ornamentation. (The metronome setting is quite fast but the feel of horas is still *andante*).

This type of hora is also called a *zhok* (street music), *krumer tants* (crooked dance) or just "slow hora" (to differentiate it from the Israeli style).

BESSARABIAN HORA

This tune is also known as *Nokh a Glezl Vayn* (*Another Glass of Wine*) and has also been recorded in A minor and C minor. This version is based on one by Belf's Romanian Orchestra ("Klezmer Pioneers" - Rounder1089).

The rhythm for the first three measures is probably rendered more accurately:

The D7 chords in parentheses in sections 1 and 3 should be played only on the second and fourth repeats.

"BOYBERIKER KHASENE" HORA

Like *Der Badkhen* later in this book, *Boyberiker Khasene* was one of a series of recordings from the first quarter of the twentieth century that fed upon sentimental memories of Jewish immigrants for life back in the Old Country. It intersperses short tunes between (sometimes satirical) scenes from a wedding celebration.

The fast runs in measures 11 and 34 are approximations of what actually goes on. Just cram them into a beat and one-half any way you can. The slide in measures 12 and 24 is quite slow, of about 1/4 note duration.

This is one of my favorites, with lots of scale shifts and plenty of space for chirps and slides. In the third part the accompanists mix in a bit of a typical waltz beat with the "1"-"3" of the hora. It can be heard on "Klezmer Music" (Global Village 104 and Folkways 34021).

60

DER GASN NIGUN (A)

The Street Tune has also been recorded under the title *National Hora*. I have transcribed two versions of this piece so you may hear how different performers interpret the kind of embellishments that are intrinsic to the hora dance form. It was the kind of tune played to accompany the bridal party home as the previous *Firn Die Mekhatonim Aheim*.

The first version is based on one by Kandel's Orchestra 1923 rendition ("Jakie Jazz 'em Up" - Global Village 101) that featured heavy duty xylophone work by Jacob Hoffman. This melody also appears as part of Max Weissman's *Doina* on the same album. It was performed in Am ("Leon Schwartz - Like a Different World" Global Village 109). There are some neat mode changes peppered through the first section. Make your instrument cry in this tune.

61

DER GASN NIGUN (B)

The second version of *Gasn Nigun* is based on Abe Schwartz's 1920 violin solo ("Klezmer Music" Folklyric 9034). Schwartz was born in Romania and was a prolific recording artist in the first generation of American klezmorim. The pace is quicker and Schwartz launches into a freylakh half-way through. The two measures before the opening double bar line of the freylakh (measures 36-37) are not a melody, but a set-up of the new tempo and rhythm.

The grace note in measure 23 takes its duration from the following note.

FIRN DIE MEKHATONIM AHEIM

This classic hora is based on Naftule Brandwein's recording ("Klezmer Music" - Folkways 34021). It also appears on albums by Zev Feldman and Andy Statman (Shanachie 21002) and the Klezmorim (Arhoolie 3011). The title translates to *Accompanying the Parents of the Bride and Groom Home.* I have notated this piece in a high register for most instruments because I feel that the shrill sound of Brandwein's setting adds a great deal to the emotional power.

In measures 4 and 54 the grace notes take time from the following note. In measure 11 the timing is sometimes closer to:

Brandwein occasionally rushes or drags the timing while always returning to a steady tempo. This is the kind of detail that highlights the fact that written notation can only augment the learning that comes with listening and watching experts playing. He is so full of inventive spunk that it is often difficult to determine the melody through the musical tinsel and spaghetti that pours out of his horn. Check out section 2. The stuttering motives build up a delicious tension but it is excruciating to attempt a musical reading without having heard this piece before. Notice that there is a general contour downwards as of measure 21, with noodling around C, then A, then F#. Measure 28 is an approximation of a burst of notes with rubbery phrasing, so do not read it literally.

At the end of each section Brandwein plays the same eight measure passage but with varying rhythm.

GYPSY HORA

This touching piece can be heard on "Zev Feldman and Andy Statman" (Shanachie 21002) featuring the latter on mandolin. There are numerous rubato-like pauses and ritards accompanied by wild swings of dynamics. Only a couple of the latter are indicated, as Statman changes these variables with each repetition.

Try to put feeling into every note of this deceptively simple tune. Make every one count.

HORA #1

This hora is abstracted from a doina/hora/sirba medley by violinist Leon Schwartz, recorded in the late 1980's ("Leon Schwartz - Like a Different World" Global Village 109). The sirba can be found in the next chapter. When following a rubato section, such as a doina, a hora is sometimes referred to as a *nokhspil* (a "postlude")[1]. The accompanists were a seconding violin and bass. The A minor accompaniment is constant through many dissonances.

That's F♯ and D♯ in the key signature, folks.

1. See the notes for this album by Michael Alpert.

HORA #2

Hora #2 is based on the playing of Leon Schwartz ("Like a Different World" - Global Village 109). It is titled "Bulgar" on the album and is part of a hora/bulgar medley.

HORA #3

This melody is an approximation of the partially rubato cornet playing on Art Schryer's Modern Jewish Orchestra ("Jakie Jazz 'em Up" Global Village 101). The piece is part of a medley recorded under the title of *Yiddeshe Doina*. Despite their presence in most of the recording klezmer groups, this is one of the few early examples of an extended solo on cornet or trumpet.

The orchestra supplies a constant rhythm for this section of the recording.

HORA FROM "BAYM REBN IN PALESTINA"

With the Rabbi in Palestine was recently recorded on "Wedding Party" (Global Village 136) by the revivalist Maxwell Street Klezmer Band. With all the glissandi they supply, the second section sounds pretty zany.

In measure 32 the notation indicates that the fall-off occurs during the third beat of the G note's duration.

ZHOK

This hora is based on the playing of Dave Tarras on a his last recording in 1979 ("Music for the Traditional Jewish Wedding" - Balkan Arts Center US 1002).

KALLARASH

This tune was learned from the album "Zev Feldman and Andy Statman" (Shanachie 21002) who played cymbalom and clarinet, respectively. Statman plays this an octave higher than notated. It can also be heard played by Naftule Brandwein on "Klezmer Music" Folklyric 9034. The phrasing of measures 1-3 and 9-11 is sometimes closer to:

The slide in measure 4 takes up approximately the second quarter note of the half note duration. Measures 32 and 34 are played by the cymbalom in answer to the clarinet solo.

73

ORIENTAL HORA (A)

This is based on a version by violinist Max Liebowitz. The cymbalom accompaniment is mostly the melody (with different embellishments) and only a hint of harmony.

The double grace note figures in measures 3, 7 and 13 should be given the feeling of a catch in the throat, a variant of the "sob effect" discussed in "Interpreting the Notation". The upper note is barely heard, but there is a definite rise in pitch after the first grace, followed by a quick downward break to the main note[1]. All these are played <u>on</u> the downbeat, taking time from the following note. (The A notes in this figure can be flat or natural.) The eighth note F♯ in measure 9 is a variation of this motive, and they can be interchanged.

The lower double graces in measures 19, 20, 37, and 38 should be interpreted similarly, but their lower pitches make for a much less obvious effect.

The phrasing of measure 5 borders on:

i.e. an even spacing of four notes over three beats.

---

1. This sound may actually be some sort of *shtick* involving the clarinet keys, without regard to exact, distinct pitches.

"ORIENTAL HORA (B) EXCERPTS"

The first section of this recording is the same as that of *Hora from "Orientalische Melody"* earlier in this chapter. This mournful number is taken from a recording by Abe Schwartz on violin with just piano accompaniment ("Klezmer Music" - Global Village 104 and Folkways 34021). Take your time on this piece. I have notated only some of the ornaments Schwartz employs.

Schwartz sometimes extends the C note for a full four measures to begin the first section. For simplicity I have labeled this part as section 1, though it is second on the recording.

YIDDISH TANZ

This beautiful hora is full of tricky timing. Max Liebowitz's violin wrings emotion out of almost every note. On the old 78 r.p.m. recording the sole accompaniment is a busy and complementary piano.

The parenthetical A notes are part of the "sob effect" mentioned many times previously. Liebowitz plays the F♯-A mini-motive with a slightly different timing and clarity on the A note. (When there is no parentheses the note is fully fingered and unambiguous.)

The many repeated notes in section 3 are made interesting by their varied timing and the pitch interruption by the grace notes. During the repeat Liebowitz plays G/B♭ double stops in measures 35-37. He omits the grace notes when doing this.

The A/D open string half notes that Liebowitz bows several times are not part of the melody, but act more as a filler between motives.

The double grace notes in measures 52 and 60 are placed <u>on</u> the down beat. The slide at the end of measure 60 takes up the last quarter note of duration.

The second half of the medley on the record is a freylakh.

"FREYLAKHS, BULGARS AND OTHER UP-TEMPO TUNES"

These are the tunes most associated with today's klezmer scene. The Eastern motives gain a wildness in Western ears when played with abandon at speedy tempos. For maximum effect it helps to have a rhythm section that knows all the typical grooves and kicks that are time tested.

Freylakh means "merriment" or "pleasure", and in a musical context refers to dances at fast tempos in 2/4 or 4/4 meter. Tunes identified as *Bulgars*[1] (or *Bulagarishes*) in their titles are often indistinguishable from freylakhs to my ears, but are said to derive from a Moldavian (or the geographically close, Bessarabian) take on a Bulgarian dance[2]. A *sher* is a "scissors" dance that, at least my mother thinks comes from Russia. The sher tunes are a relatively old part of the klezmer repertoire. Old recordings titled "shers" were usually medleys of many short tunes. Rhythmically they were performed like freylakhs.

1. The accent is on the second syllable.

2. See Michael Alpert's notes to Leon Schwart'z album, *Like a Different World* (Global Village #109). The development of the bulgar is discussed in depth in Walter Feldman's article "The Transformation of a Klezmer Dance Genre." (See "Bibliography.") The latter makes a case for a specific bulgar-type cadence and the more frequent appearance of triplets. It is unclear if the latter is born out in the transcriptions in this book. What some might interpret as 1/4 note triplets, I feel are actually phrased as some combination of two 1/16's and an 1/8.

DER BADKHEN FREYLAKH

A badkhen used to be employed as a combination master of ceremonies, prankster, musician and ad hoc poet for festive affairs, especially weddings. This piece is based on a humorous look at a badkhen's work, by H. L. Reismann (who probably was the badkhen on the record). The melody is carried by violin with piano accompaniment. In measures 9 and 13, the 1/32 note figure can be played as a 1/32 triplet, adding another 1/32 B after the C note.

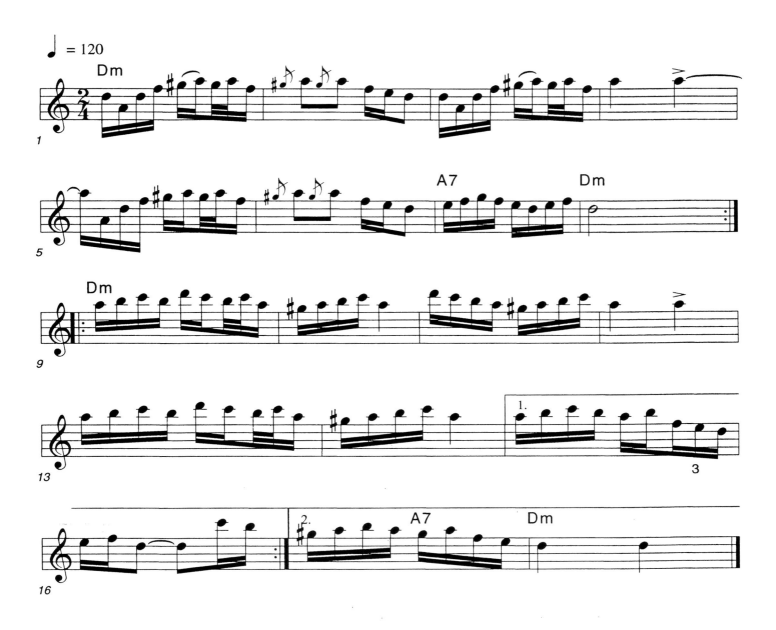

79

BEHUSHER KHOSID

Max Liebowitz was a member of the first generation of klezmorim to be recorded so his performance might represent quite an old violin style. I hear quite a bit of Romanian Gypsy in some of his work on *Behusher Khosid*. The accompaniment by cymbalom is an unrelenting series of unaccented 1 and 5 steps of the chords. For example:

The *pizz.* refers to plucking the violin strings and *arco* indicates to return to bowing. The other violin-istic touches are the double stops in section 2. The kind of syncopated rhythm in the latter part of section 2 is unique to any old klezmer performance that I have heard.

The first B notes of measures 30 and 31 may have been split into the B and a partially fingered D above, to give the catch-in-the-throat effect. The first 8 measures of section 3 are remindful of the kind of flourish heard in sirbas.

Note that section 4 is played three times. After the third repeat return to the beginning. The first measure of the coda is an approximation of the indistinct smear of notes that Liebowitz plays.

"BEIM REBBEN'S TISH" EXCERPTS

At the Rabbi's Table is from Dave Tarras' long deleted "Freylakh in Hi-Fi" album from the 1950's. It featured the kind of 4-5 person ensemble of clarinet, trap set, brass and accordion that Tarras made the standard of klezmorim in the United States. It was not until the revival that began in earnest in the late 1970's that the pre-1940 sound was re-invigorated.

BESSARABIER KHOSIDL

Versions of this *Khosidl from Bessarabia* are currently available on "Klezmer Pioneers" on Rounder 1089 and Kapelye's "Future and Past" album on Flying Fish 249.

When section 1 is repeated, measures 15 and 16 are altered and the last four measures are omitted. Measures 3, 6, 37, and 44 feature the quick, "whimpering" doublet (here sixteenth notes) form that I mentioned in *Orientalische Melody Hora*. The second, higher note of the doublets are played somewhat shorter than the first in this piece. You can phrase them as double grace notes if you wish, extending the following note to make up for the shortening of the first two.

The third section is suspiciously un-Oriental, perhaps borrowed from a once current West European "art" melody.

BOYBERIKER KHASENE MELODIES

These four melodies were placed in the midst of a recorded skit about an old country-style wedding ("Klezmer Music" - Global Village 104 and Folkways 34021). It was performed by the Boyberiker Kapelye, named for a town from the old country. They were not played consecutively, but had dialogue between them.

The third one is announced as a wedding march, but the mekhatonim would have to sprint down the aisle at the chosen tempo. The first full four measures of this part are an introduction.

#1

#2

FISELEKH, FISELEKH

Presaging the rock group of the same name, *Little Feet* was recorded in 1915 by Elenkrig's Orchestra ("Klezmer Music" - Folklyric 9034). As usual, the clarinet pipes up an octave above this notation. See the similar "A Laibediga Honga". Measures 16-17 are rhythmic filler.

FLASKADRIGA

I learned this tune from Andy Statman, a moving force in the new generation of klezmer-ites that revived this music for the public.

When I asked my Yiddish sources for a definition of *Flaskadriga* I was told, *P'chech* (the 'ch' pronounced as in `cheek'). When asked about *p'chech* I heard, "Sort of a whiner, a *tsatsgaleh*. That in turn produced, "A toy, but really more like a *veybele mit un earing'l* (spoken in the best Yinglish). That of course is a "wife with an earing", but what has that to do with *tsatsgaleh*, *p'chech* or even *flaskadriga*? Actually it is obvious. It is someone who is *"fency, shmency* but shrewd as a fox". What is the definition of *flaskadriga*? Please don't ask.

FON DER KHUPE #1

From the Wedding Canopy #1 is based on Dave Tarras's playing on ("Music for the Traditional Jewish Wedding" - Balkan Arts Center US 1002). It might have been in the key of F on the record.

FON DER KHUPE #2

From the Wedding Canopy #2 has been recorded from medium speed wedding march to freylakh overdrive. It is based on performances by Abe Elenkrig's Orchestra ("Klezmer Pioneers" - Rounder 1089), The Klezmorim ("Streets of Gold" - Arhoolie 3011) where it is recorded as "Silver Wedding"), and Abe Schwartz's Orchestra (Master of Klezmer Music - Volume One" - Global Village 126) where it is titled *Die Ziberne Khassene*.

Section 2 is the "hook" of this piece with both melodic and rhythmic excitement. The optional harmony notes are in small print. The triplets serve as a relaxant after the shock of the series of accented stops that precede them. Begin this section with a crescendo during the rising scale passage. (There is a similar section in *Der Berdichiever Khosid* in the chapter of khosidls.)

Section 3 is typical of a family of "section 3's" that are melodically plain, and need (in my opinion) some hard driving rhythm to keep it interesting. (See also *Odessa Bulgar #1* and *Ma Yofus*.)

Though very high pitched, I recommend playing this an octave higher.

FREITAG NOKHN TSIMMES

This version is based on the 1919 recording by the Joseph Frankel Orchestra ("Jakie Jazz 'em Up" Global Village 101). It may have actually been played in C minor. The clarinet player chirps and trills maniacally over the entire third section.

The title roughly translates to *Friday After the Tsimmes*. The latter is something like a vegetable and/or fruit pudding served with the main course. In the Bronx, *tsimes* was usually made with carrots.

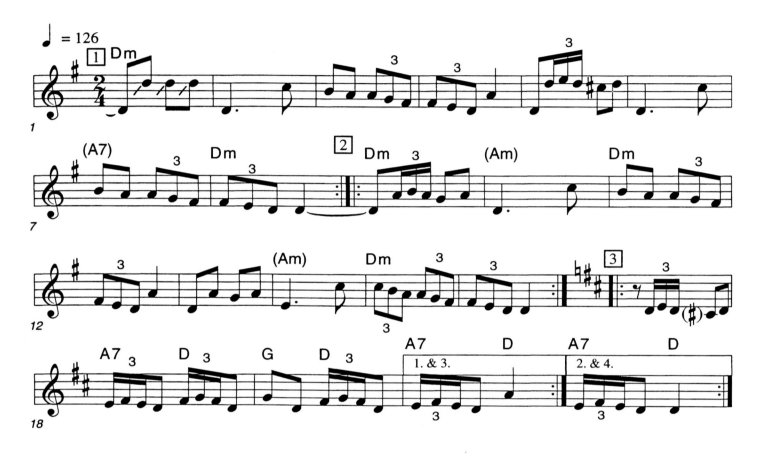

92

FREYLAKH FROM "DIE MAME IS GEGANGEN IN MARK AREYN"

This excerpt from *The Mother is Going to Market* is based on the recording by the revival band, Kapelye on their album "Future and Past" (Flying Fish 249). The title of the group means "band" in Yiddish.

In section 2 the backup plays a lot of the typical freylakh rhythm kick:

Section 3 is very Western sounding and features wood blocks' playing figures like:

I have heard that the only reason wood blocks were used on the old 78 r.p.m. recordings was that they could cut through the other instruments and be picked up by the primitive microphones of the time. Now they have become a standard feature of modern klezmer-type bands.

FREYLAKH FROM "DOINA" MEDLEY #1

Violinist Leon Ahl played this freylakh after an extended doina on an old 78 r.p.m. record. The difference between the grace notes in measure 2, the 1/32 note triplet in measure 3, and the two 1/32 notes followed by a 1/16 that ends measure 3 may, in actuality, only be the way I interpreted an old, scratchy record.

The "flourish" motive that begins section 2 is recorded an octave higher. The grace notes are placed <u>on</u> the downbeats in these four measures. The parenthetical E note in section 2 is a ghosted note; part of the klezmer-style "sob-effect".

The third and fourth sections have phrasing and melodic contours like a sirba. I have placed a couple of C♯'s in parentheses when the exact pitch was indistinct on the recording. The C natural is a courtesy accidental.

94

FREYLAKH FROM "FUN TASHLIKH"

This tune is part of a medley apparently related to the Jewish observance of *tashlikh*, the New Year's ritual ridding of sins. It was recorded by Kapelye on "Future and Past" (Flying Fish 249). It might be more accurate to call this a sirba what with the continuous sixteenth note quality of this arrangement. It has some interesting shifts between modes with G natural, A flat and A natural.

FREYLAKH FROM "ROMANIAN DOINA"

This *freylakh* is the last tune played on a recording of a medley by Abe Schwartz on violin ("Klezmer Music" - Global Village 104 and Folkways 34021). The pianist insists on an Am chord to accompany measures 3-4, while the melody strongly suggests Gm to me.

The first two measures are a short interlude, a bit like a brass fanfare, that is typical of some Romanian folk instrumental music. The slide in measure 18 begins on the down beat and is continuous and slow.

The harmonic "A"s sound an octave higher.

FREYLAKH IN D

Freylakh in D is from a recording by Klezmer Plus and is an excerpt of a medley of freylakhs after an extended *doina* and *hora* interlude. It has the sort of melody that grabs hold immediately.

In measures 1 and 5 the timing difference between the two 1/16-1/8 and the quarter note triplet is not worth worrying over. Divide the timing of each beat either way or somewhere between. At the suggested tempo it goes by too quickly to worry about it.

Play the second section four times.

DER GLATER BULGAR

The Plain or *"Simple" (more literally " Smooth") Bulgar* is based on the playing of Dave Tarras ("Klezmer Music" - Global Village 104 and Folkways 34021). Though set at freylakh speed the rhythm by the accompanying accordion and trap set seems more like a khosidl.

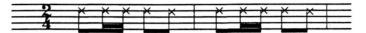

The second section is filled with delicious scalar modulations. They make for wide leeway in choosing chords. The first and third sections are in the kind of key signatures you rarely see in pop or country music.

HEYMISH FREYLAKH

Violinist Max Liebowitz recorded *Home-y Freylakh* as the second of a two part medley titled "Yiddish Hora". The cymbalom accompanist does play the parenthetical D minor chord with each pass, and quite a tangy touch it is. I take ultimate responsibility for the parenthetical A7.

The last seven notes of measure 25 is an approximation of the scalar smear of notes that Liebowitz squeezes into 1 1/2 beats. In measures 26-29 the cymbalom halts its obbligato accompaniment to play

This suggests an atypical harmony, at least by Western art music standards.

I hope more of the work of this excellent klezmer violinist will soon be reissued.

100

KHASENE MARCH #1

This tune can be found on "Zev Feldman and Andy Statman" (Shanachie 21002). Despite the title it is too fast to be a march and is recorded with the rhythmic feel of a freylakh.

KHOSEN KALE MAZEL TOV

Congratulations to the Bride and Groom is a wedding standard though the second and third sections in this arrangement are somewhat rare. Examples can be heard on Gus Goldstein's *Der Mesader Kedushin"* or *The Wedding Master* ("Jakie Jazz 'em Up" - Global Village 101), Harry Kandel's Orchestra ("Harry Kandel - Russian Sher" - Global Village 128), and Lou Lockett's Orchestra ("Dave Tarras" - Yazoo 7001).

Nowadays many sing this with all A naturals. However, for me, it is just those accidentals that make this tune a superior piece.

102

KISHNIEV #2

This is the second half of a medley as played by Dave Tarras ("Music for the Traditional Jewish Wedding" - Balkan Arts Center US 1002). The first part is in the chapter of khosidls and terkeshes. Though the tempo is just a bit quicker than *Kishniev #1*, the freylakh rhythm is played by the accompanying accordion and drums. The typical rhythm kick is something like:

Kishniev #2 is another example of Dave Tarras' subtle artistry of weaving from one mode to the other. After a couple of choruses of this Tarras performs *Kishniev #1* in the same rhythm.

KOLOMEYKE

Kolomeyke is a town in the Galician region of the Ukraine. Doctor Feldman says it is also a Ruthenian dance. According to the notes for the album, "Leon Schwartz - Like a Different World" (Global Village 109), this is actually a combination of two other tunes. The first two sections are derived from one titled *Verkhovyna"* the name of a region of the Carpathian Mountains. The third section is *Honyl Viter*, a Ukranian tune translated as *Howling Wind*. In the latter I am reasonably sure that Schwartz meant to play E naturals, but they sound a bit strange.

LEBIDIKH UN FREYLAKH

Having trouble waking up in the morning? Abe Schwartz's rendition of this tune ("Klezmer Music" - Global Village 104 and Folkways 34021) is the perfect antidote. (It was also recorded by the Klezmorim on "Streets of Gold" - Arhoolie 3011.) *Lively and Happy* is mighty jazzy and peppy. The arrangement of the bass lines as played by the brass on the recording (not notated here) is intrinsic to the high energy of the tune.

The first two measures are an introduction, played only once. You might wish to chirp the first three notes of measure 39 for a cheery, laughing sound. There are several unrelated tunes recorded under the same tittle.

KOLYN

Coals is based on Mishka Tsiganoff's accordion solo from 1919 on "Jakie Jazz 'em Up" (Global Village 101). Though he speeds up, as reflected in the tempo range, the general feel is relaxed and constrained. The third section is the same as the third section of *Vu Bist Du Geveyzen fur Prohibish* transcribed later in this chapter.

According to the album notes, Tsiganoff also recorded for Russian, Polish, Ukranian, and Romanian audiences, each time translating his last name (Gypsy) to the appropriate language.

A LAIBEDIGA HONGA

A Lively Honga Dance is based on the Kandel's Orchestra 1925 recording ("Klezmer Pioneers" Rounder 1089). Clarinet player Harry Kandel, a native of Poland was one of the first generation of klezmorim in America, though he played American popular music for many years before an audience grew sufficiently large to support klezmer and other music of the Jewish immigrants from Central and Eastern Europe.

Whatever sort of dance a *honga* is, its musical form is very much like the *shers* transcribed later in this section.

The alternate version of section 3 omits the first four measures of the first section 3. It is played in the position shown, directly after section 4. After 3' repeat section 4.

Repeat ④ then *D.C. al fine*

LIEBES TANZ

Dance of Love is based on the Abe Schwartz Orchestra recording of 1916 ("Klezmer Pioneers" - Rounder 1089). For the Romanian market it was titled *Ai raci ku ne draci*. It is on the borderline between an up-tempo freylakh and khupe march.

Play the entire first section (with inner repeats) twice before continuing.

Occasionally measures 15 and 23-24 are played as C minor. In the sections 2 and 3, play the G7 chord on the second and fourth repetitions. Play section 5 four times.

MAMALIGA

A *mamaliga* is a Romanian style corn meal pudding. This musical recipe is based on a 1923 effort by Harry Kandel's Orchestra ("Jakie Jazz 'em Up" Global Village 101).

You might consider short slides up to the first four notes. The G notes that begin the second section may be played an octave lower. On the record a piccolo trilled as a high as possible D note during measures 21-24, and 29-32. In those same measures the quarter note E's are usually trilled.

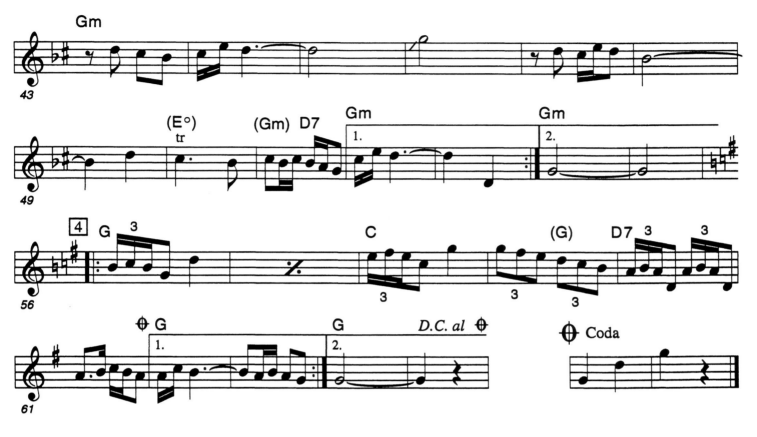

MA YOFUS

This is one of the most famous of klezmer tunes. Besides this title of *How Beautiful* it can be heard under such names as *Reb Dovidl Nigun (Rabbi David's Tune)*, *Der Rebbe Hut Gehesen Freylakh Sein (The Rabbi Has Asked Us to Make Merry)*, and *Tanz Yidelakh (Dance, Little Jew)*. It is currently available by various performers on "Klezmer Music" (Folklyric 9034), "Klezmer Pioneers" (Rounder 1089), Andy Statman and David Grisman's "Songs of Our Fathers" (Acoustic Disc 14) and "Abe Schwartz" (Global Village 126).

The lyrics for "Der Rebbe Hut Geheysen Freylakh Sein", translated from Yiddish, are something like:

"The Rabbi is making merry,
Drinking schnaps not wine".

I learned this melody from Alan Kaufman, a member of perhaps the immediate precursor of the klezmer revival, "Way of the World". (This was also the only band ever to use a Hawaiian guitar on such music.) He was about to perform it as his entry in an old time fiddle contest. Needless to say, he did not place.

Compare this with the Ukranian version in the chapter on "Related Genres of Music".

This tune is also played in the keys of E and A.

MAZEL TOV #1

Congratulations (literally, *Good Luck*) #1 is based on the Abe Schwartz recording ("Master of Klezmer Music - Volume One" Global Village 126). The clarinet and violins play an octave above the transcribed notation while the trumpet plays as written.

MAZEL TOV #2

This arrangement is based on the recording on "Andy Statman Orchestra" (Shanachie 21004). On the album the trumpet plays in the indicated register, while the clarinet tweets an octave higher.

The order of sections is 1-1-2-2-1-3-3. The first two notes of measure 3 can be chirped.

MOSHE EMES

Moses Is True comes from the recent recording "Songs of Our Fathers" (Acoustic Disc 14) that featured Andy Statman on clarinet and David Grisman on mandolin. It is another Chassidic tune (see *Nigun*) that neatly fits into klezmer repertoire. [Also see Statman's comments about this in his interview.]

The grace notes in measures 2 and 6 should be played <u>on</u> the down beat. The clarinet holds a high E note throughout the repeat of section 2. The order of sections is 1-2-3-2.

MELODIES FROM "DOINA" MEDLEY #2

The following are the two up tempo numbers from cymbalomist Joseph Moskowitz's 1916 recording ("Klezmer Pioneers" - Rounder 1089). Notice the difference in meter between them. I am not sure if this is technically correct but it reads easiest this way for me.

In the second section of tune #1, the eighth notes are swung, ie. tied triplet feel. After this tune Moskowitz stops for a moment, then kicks off #2 at a faster tempo in cut time.

The second tune seems more like a sirba than a freylakh. (I think of a sirba to be a very fast piece played with almost all straight sixteenth notes, with occasional triplet passages. Not surprisingly, there are more precise definitions. See the Walter Zev Feldman reference in "Bibliography",) Sections 3 and 4 of tune #2 are arranged with Moskowitz's cymbalom in mind.

#1

#2

DER NIKLAYVER BULGAR

Der Niklayver Bulgar comes from a 1918 recording by Harry Kandel's Orchestra now available on "Harry Kandel - Russian Sher" (Global Village 128). The first section was recorded by Cherniavsky's Yiddish-American Jazz Band under the title *Der Heyser ("Hot") Bulgar*. Doctor Feldman has identified part of that tune as the same as a Greek *hassapiko* type dance.

By now you should recognize the typical flourish-like introduction in section 2. As in many other up tempo tunes in this chapter, the first motive is one measure long and repeated. In the next two measures the duration of the motive is halved so that it takes four of the new motives to fill the next two measures. The clarinet plays this an octave above the transcribed pitches.

ODESSA BULGAR #1

This is one of the most popular tunes of the klezmer revival. It is another tune I learned at an Andy Statman concert. It appears on Kapelye's "Future and Past" (Flying Fish 249) and by Abe Schwartz's Orchestra on "Jakie Jazz 'em Up" (Global Village 101). The latter pulls out all the dampers on the third section.

I like to begin section 2 very quietly and quickly crescendo to a climax on the down beat of the third measure of that part. Play this with a wild abandon.

ODESSA BULGAR #2

This transcription id based on Mishka Tsiganoff's accordion solo of 1920 ("Klezmer Pioneers" - Rounder 1089). He exhibits no jazzy influences, playing with a sparse, almost austere approach.

After completing section 1 repeat the entire section, this time going to the alternate last measure. To end the tune go to the coda indicated at measure 14.

ODESSA BULGAR #3

This entry is from Kapelye's "Future and Past" (Flying Fish 249). It is transcribed an octave below the clarinet solo.

The actual melody in measures 25-26 is probably a four beat C note. This phrase is a buzzing embellishment. The band bursts into maximum freylakh drive in section 3. In measure 39 play the gliss down from the B♭ on the last 1/8 note of its duration.

OY TAT S'IZ GUT

Oh Father, It's Good showcases another magical mystery tour on the clarinet of Naftule Brandwein. He recorded this in 1925, while at the top of his powers ("Klezmer Music" Folklyric 9034). There are many variations with each repetition, especially in section 3 where Brandwein throws in the kitchen sink by the end of the last refrain. While not being the perfectionist that Dave Tarras was, his inventiveness, biting tone, rhythmic control, and strain of reckless wildness combine to make him my favorite klezmer.

The modal and rhythmic shift that begins section 2 is especially effective. Brandwein expresses the triplet figures with stacatto phrasing.

DEM REBEN'S NIGUN

This version of *The Rabbi's Tune* was recorded 1915 by Elenkrig's Orchestra ("Klezmer Music" - Folklyric 9034). More recently it was recorded by the the Klezmorim ("East Side Wedding" - Arhoolie 3006). It has little of the Eastern-influenced mode changes of which I am so fond. Still on the old recording, the clarinet, playing an octave higher than notated, commits a multitude of slides and chirps to locate this definitely in the klezmer repertoire. According to Martin Schwartz's notes on the album, it is a variant of an old Odessan thieves' song.

Measure 13 features another "voice-like" break in the 1/16 note figure.

RUSHISHE SHER #2(A)

This title has also served as a catch-all for medleys of many short motives. Abe Schwartz's Orchestra recorded several related pieces. It can be heard on "Klezmer Music" (Global Village 104 and Folkways 34021) and "Abe Schwartz - Volume One" (Global Village 126). Parts of it were included in a recording by Harry Kandel titled *Freylakh Mekhatonim*. This version contains some wild and wonderful melodies.

The grace notes in measures 10, ll, 30 take time from the following note.

The contour of section 3 is a motive that you will hear frequently in old klezmer music. (Also see measures 28 and 32 for example.) The clarinet sometimes trills a high D for the entirety of this section.

In section 4, measures 26-27 and, the rhythm section stops, returning on the down beat of the next measure. Their is a similar stop on the first beat of the second ending of section 6. The accompaniment returns with a bang on next measure. The slides after the first repeat of section 6 are wide and wacky. This is definitely not part of the melody, but a energy boost into the repeat of this part.

Because it involves such high pitches I decided to notate the seventh section an octave lower than played. Dig the striking key change into section 9. The particular ending point is determined more by the time requirements of the old 78 r.p.m. record format than any intrinsic form of the tune. And now - full tilt klezmer ahoy!

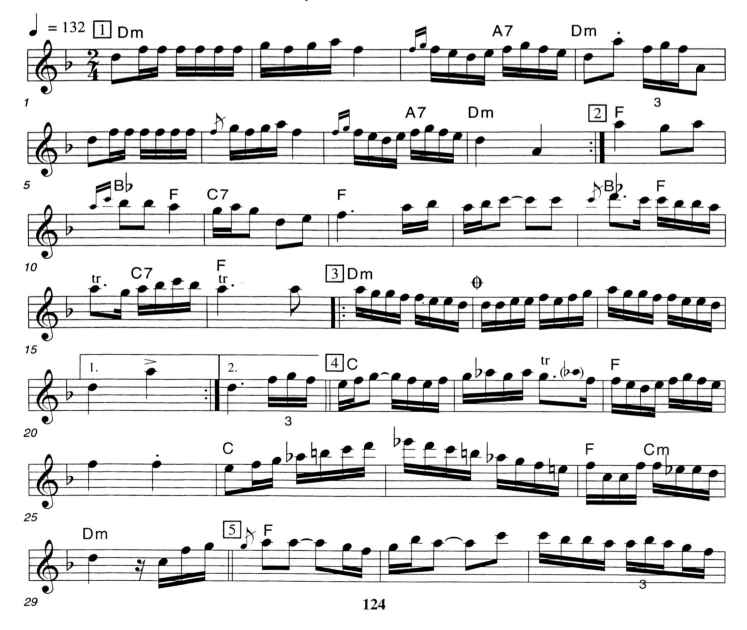

Here are some variations for *Rushishe Sher #2(A)*, based on the playing of Dave Tarras. The first four measures might be played:

The first measure of section 3:

The scale bending run of measures 26-27 can be varied to:

126

RUSHISHE SHER #2(B)

Dave Tarras recorded a similar version of this medley on his long out-of-print "Freylakh in Hi-Fi" album. Tarras shares honors with Naftule Brandwein as the most respected klezmer clarinet player on record. Here are some sections he played in his version of *Rushishe Sher* not present in Schwartz's version. Tarras recorded it in C minor and I transposed it for ease of comparison.

On the repeat of section 4 Tarras warbles a high D note for the first four measures.

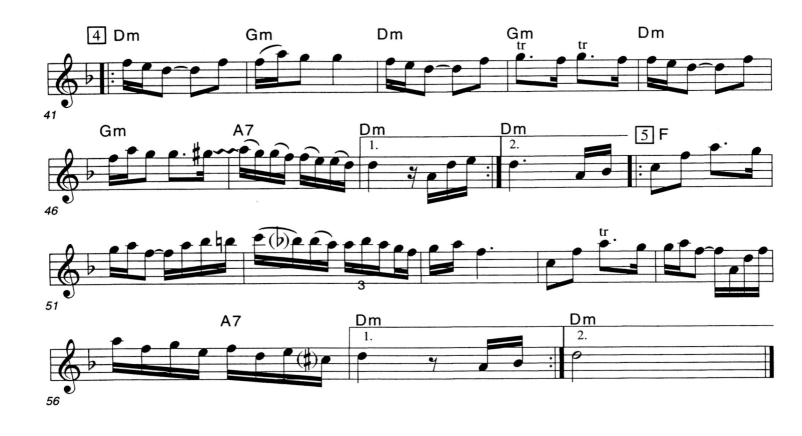

RUSHISHE SHER 2(C)

The Klezmatics recorded the following melodies before launching into the first few sections of *Rushishe Sher 2 (A)* ("Shvaygn = Toyt" - no label).

RUSIHISHE SHER 2(D)

After duplication of a few sections of *Rushishe Sher #2(A♪)*, Harry Kandel's 1917 recording offered the following melodies ("Harry Kandel - Russian Sher" - Global Village 128). The grace notes in measure 38 are <u>on</u> the downbeat.

RUSHISHE SHER #3

Abe Schwartz recorded another series of rollicking tune-lets under the same title in 1920 ("Klezmer Music" - Folklyric 9034). Play the entire form of part 6 twice.

The sher is usually referred to as a Russian 'scissors' dance although it apparently is a Jewish take on an old German dance. Ask your local scissors dancer for details.

RUSHISHE SHER #4

This medley of tunes was recorded by Kapelye "Future and Past" (Flying Fish 249) under the title, "Abe Schwartz's Famous Sher". Like the preceding pieces in this series, this entry is filled with short, lively tunes that gradually change mode.

During measures 5-6 the accompanists play:

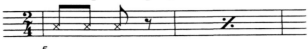

The first four measures of section 7 are accented by the accompanists:

Section 3 is particularly catchy. The clarinet plays an octave higher than notated in this section (not the whole piece). Section 8 is an up-tempo version of section of 1 in *Rushishe Sher #1* found in the "Khosidl" section of this book. Note the substitution of F natural for the F sharp of *Rushishe Sher #1* in the third measure of section 8.

After section 8 Kapelye launches into sections 9, 10 and ending on, 11 from *Rushishe Sher #2*.

135

RUSHISHE SHER #5

This is the Harry Kandel collection of sher melodies ("Harry Kandel - Russian Sher" - Global Village 128). It was recorded in 1917 under the title *Russian Sher Part One*. The grace notes are phrased on the down beats. In measures 33 and 41 the accompanists interrupt the rhythm groove, hit an accent on the second beat and hold until the next measure.

The tricky rhythm in measure 36 is sometimes played in other motives in this transcription with similar contours like measures 34,38-39 and 51. Following section 5 the band plays section 1-4 of *Rushishe Sher #3*.

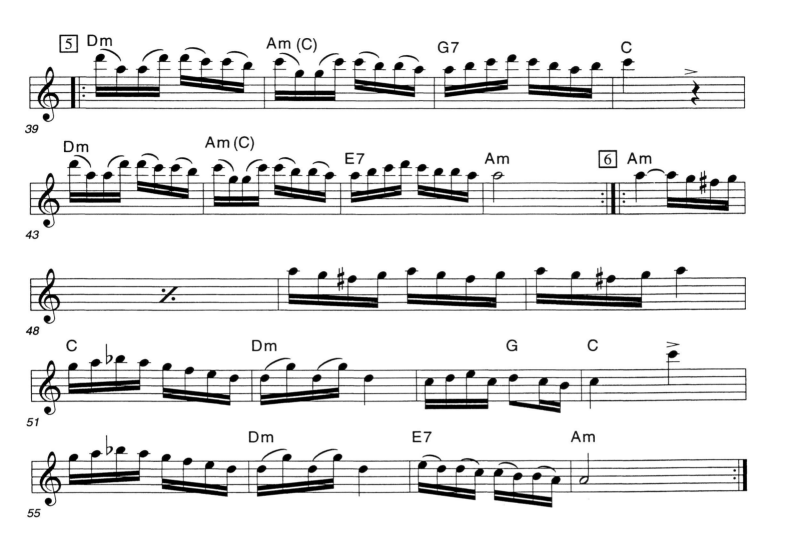

RUSISHE KAMARINSKA

The Russian Kamarinska (another type of dance) is adapted from a 1921 recording by the Harry Kandel Orchestra ("Harry Kandel - Russian Sher" - Global Village 128). Except for the flourishes it sounds pretty close to a typical fiddle tune from the southeast of the United States. The slightly skewed phrasing in parts 1 and 2, where the melody is only three measures long is also reminiscent of a phylum of American fiddle tunes.

138

RUSSIAN BULGAR

This spiffy bulgar (accent on the last syllable) was recorded by the Abe Schwartz Orchestra ("Master of Klezmer Music - Volume One" Global Village 126). The third section shows the influence of military march music.

SADEGER KHOSID

Sadeger (now called Sadgora) is a town in The Ukraine. This tune is based on the cymbalom offerings of Joseph Moskowitz, recorded in 1916, and so represents the un-Americanized sound of klezmer ("Klezmer Music" Folklyric 9034). The cymbalom has little sustain, so there are relatively many notes of short duration in this piece. Instead of letting a note ring, it is played several times in succession like a tremolo on a mandolin. (See measures 21-22.)

There are some exciting modal shifts in sections 5 and 6. Compare this section 5 with the second section of *Tate Siser* later in this chapter.

DER SHTILER BULGAR

The Quiet Bulgar is probably the most famous klezmer melody in America, having served as the basis for the Benny Goodman Orchestra's hit of 1939, *And the Angels Sing*. It was contributed by one of his trumpeters, an ex-klezmerite, Ziggy Elman. This version is mostly based on the recording by the Abe Schwartz Orchestra in 1918 ("Klezmer Music" - Folklyric 9034).

The variations of the second section are based on Kandel's Orchestra's *Jakie Jazz 'Em Up* ("Jakie Jazz 'em Up" - Global Village 101) and one of the melodies on *Oriental Melody* by Max Liebowitz (who played it in the key of G). It is also known as *Zol Zayn Freylakh* (*Let There Be Joy*).

141

TATE SISER

Sweet Father was recorded by the Abe Schwartz Orchestra ("Master of Klezmer Music - Volume One" Global Village 126). Another version was recorded by Liebowitz's Yiddish Orchestra under the title *Die Silbere Hochzeit* (*The Silver Anniversary*). The modulation from the D major of section 1 to the F major of section 2 helps make the latter very catchy. In section 3 the clarinet chirps and trills an octave higher than the melody while the percussionist goes wild on the cymbals, emphasizing:

SIRBA #1

I learned this piece at a concert by the Andy Statman Orchestra I do not have a recording, but
I remember the tempo to be approximately as noted. ,

SIRBA #2

This sirba is excerpted from a doina/hora/sirba medley performed by violinist Leon Schwartz in the late 1980's ("Leon Schwartz - Like a Different World" Global Village 109).

In practice, the triplet passages are often phrased as two sixteenths followed by an eighth. The stratospheric stuff beginning measures 44, 46, etc. are F♯-G♯-F♯ sixteenth note triplets followed by an E note.

The high D♯ grace notes beginning in measure 53 should be played <u>on</u> the downbeats.

It is reminiscent of the type of folk melody that was usurped by art composers as part of a Hungarian rhapsody or something of the like. You need to be a bit of a virtuoso to really cut this one.

D.C. al Fine

SIRBA #3

This is simply titled *Sirba* on Leon Schwartz's "Like a Different World" Global Village 109. The order of sections is 1-2-1-3-2.

SIRBA #4

Dave Tarras plays this peppy number on "Music for the Traditional Jewish Wedding" (Balkan Arts Center US 1002). Though called a sirba it lacks that genre's typical triplets.

The mix of the natural and sharp forms of D and F notes is the coolest. The key signature for section 2 is F# and D#.

VU BIST DU GEVEYZEN FUR PROHIBISH

Where Were You Before Prohibition? is a perfect set up for the genius of Naftule Brandwein ("Klezmer Music" - Global Village 104 and Folkways 34021). He chirps, slides, trills, sputters and toys with the rhythm, floating with seemingly complete abandon through this virtuosic exercise. What is the key signature? The B naturals are in parentheses because he glosses over this pitch, leaving it open to interpretation. Brandwein does many variations with each repeat, so the following is represents only one pass through the form.

The double grace notes are phrased <u>on</u> the beat, borrowing time from the following note.

In part 3, the clarinet swoops down <u>almost</u> to a high C♯ and immediately skips back up to D, as if the C♯ was too hot to touch. The exact pitch is not critical as long as the sense of falling and rising is discernible. The same holds true for the business in measures 43-44 and 50-51.

I decided to keep his playing in the actual octave because much of the delicious tension is lost at lower pitches. Instruct your percussionist to bash away on the cymbals on most of the "1" and "+" (after "2") beats.

Brandwein was born in Galicia and was not recorded much after the 1920's.

SIRBA #5

This tune was recorded around 1920 as part of Israel Chazin's flute solo on *Doina and Sirba*. This instrument was once a focal part of klezmer bands but lost its status with the ascendency of brass and it's inability to be heard above the latter in early recording studios.

Chazin's style shows the influence of Western art music and the pace is a bit slower than the other sirbas, probably to allow his dense cascade of notes. The grace notes in measures 1, 2 and 4 are placed on the downbeat. The timing in measure 11 is just an approximation of the smear of notes Chazin plays.

RELATED GENRES OF MUSIC

THE FOLK MUSIC OF NON-JEWS OF EASTERN EUROPE

The music now known as klezmer both influenced and was influenced by the surrounding non-Jewish communities. Klezmorim played for gentiles and vice-versa, indicating the opportunity for plenty of musical trading. The transcriptions in this chapter should help you understand the essence of klezmer by comparison with other instrumental folk music of Central and Eastern Europe. These selections may not be representative of their region. I chose them both for their beauty and because each evinced some sort of similarity to klezmer performances - in approach to use of scales, melodic contour, "Oriental" influence, instrumentation, etc. (However see Doctor Feldman's corrective to my musings in the interview that follows this chapter.)

The societal status of Gypsies has some similarity to the situation of pre-World War II Jewry: ostracized from the mainstream (often with governmental sanction), feared and held in contempt by the mass of the population, living a ghetto-ized areas, and valued by the mainstream for their musical abilities. As Henry Sapoznik has written:

> "Sharing as they [Jews and Gypsies] did a common perception of Europe,
> independent of political boundaries, the musicians of both these communities
> also shared an antipathy to the judgmental, heavy hand of other Europeans.
> Religion, mobility and quintessential "otherness" as well as a strong feeling
> for each other's music, did much to provoke a meaningful musical symbiosis
> between these two ethnic minorities,"   [See Bibliography for reference.]

BIRLADEANCA

Ian Dragoi is one of the great practitioners of gypsy-style Romanian violin. This transcription is based on his now out-of-print Electrochord album (#STS-EPE 0776). He handles this virtuosic piece at a frightening tempo with relaxed aplomb. Since many of the older klezmer recordings were of Jewish music from this part of the world (though somewhat to the west), it may be instructive to compare these "folk" musics.

Dragoi is accompanied by an equally invincible cymbalom player. The accompanying chords are my invention. A closer approximation of his noting of measures 6-8 , but measurably more difficult to handle, is given in the following example.

A closer reading of measures 24-25 gives:

152

DANCE FROM MÁRAMAROS

This tune was recorded by Hungarian Gypsies who used to play for Jewish communities before World War II. The title refers to a town in Transylvania. This performance can be heard on "Muzsikás - The Lost Jewish Music of Transylvania" (Hannibal 1373). It was performed by Árpád Toni on cymbalom.

HORA DE LA MOINESTI

This effort by Ian Dragoi is obviously not the Rumanian type of hora referred to in the "Hora" chapter. The modal manipulations are mind boggling. I am reasonably sure this is what Ian Dragoi plays, taken from the same album as *Birladeanca*. The identity of the F notes in the second section gets murky. Try different combinations of natural and sharp. It is just the "folk process" in action.

The down slides off the D notes are a lazy sort of fall-off of about a half-step and a quarter note duration.

The basic cymbalom accompaniment is:

Again, the chords are my own interpretations of some of the harmonic possibilities of this piece.

IVANKO

Ivanko is from the album "Wedding Party" (Global Village 136) by the revivalist Maxwell Street Klezmer Band. It apparently was learned from a recent Russian émigré and band member. The liner notes describe it as "typical Ukrainian folk song...popular at Russian-Jewish celebrations since the 1930's". There is little, if any, Eastern influence in the performance. The harmonies were played on accordion. How this tune and performance are related to the sound of Jewish music before the destruction of Jewish enclaves in western Russia can only be guessed.

JEWISH DANCE FROM SZÁSZRÉGEN

The title of this piece from "Muzsikás - The Lost Jewish Music of Transylvania" (Hannibal 1373) refers to a pre-World War II Jewish community. According to the album notes by Judit Frigyesi, this was originally a rubato piece recorded here in a rhythm reminiscent of a tango. This is not unheard of in Chassidic circles. (See "Nigun" in the chapter on *khosidls*.) On the record it is performed on cymbalom. It has the same melody as "Belz", a mournful Yiddish song about the town of that name.

KHOSID DANCE

This tune is adapted from the violin playing of Csaba Okros on "Muzsikás - The Lost Jewish Music of Transylvania" (Hannibal 1373). The melody was accompanied by the drones and strums of various stringed instruments in gypsy style. The overall structure and tempo of this piece is related to a *freylakh* but it is performed closer to the local style of csárdás. That is, the effect is more Hungarian than klezmer.

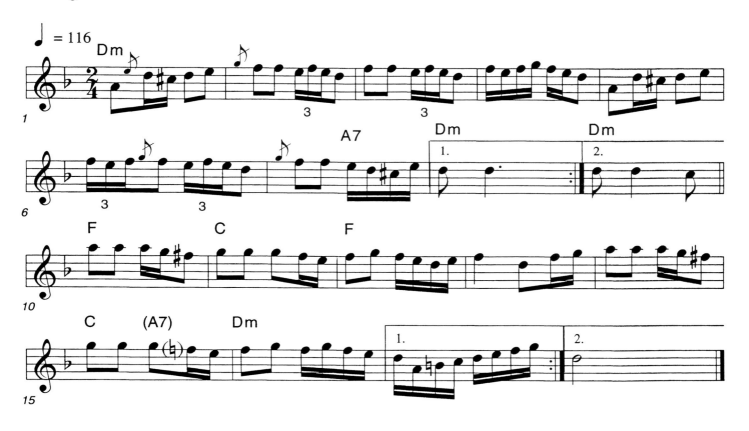

KHOSID WEDDING DANCE

Here is another tune from "Muzsikás - The Lost Jewish Music of Transylvania" (Hannibal 1373). It is similar in feel and performance to the preceding piece.

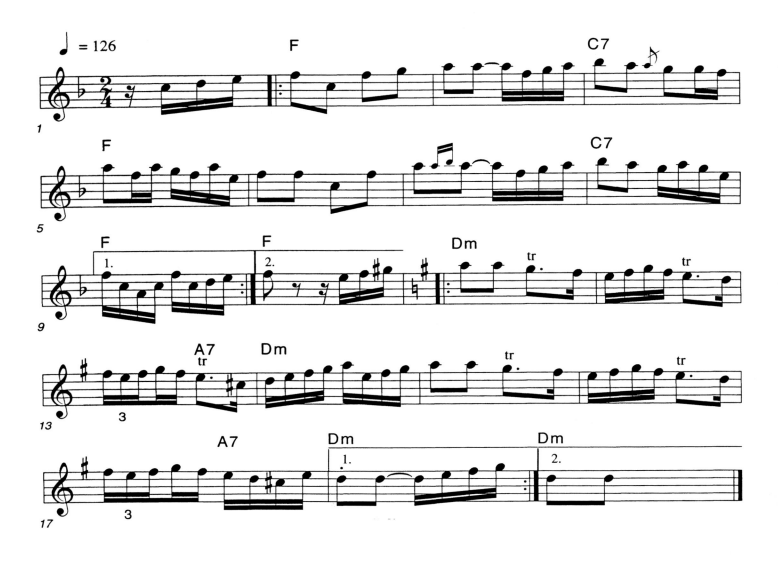

OJ PIDU JA SZICHER WICHER

This is a Ukrainian version of *Ma Yofus* (see "Freylakh" chapter) played by violinist Pawlo Humeniuk in 1927 with accordion accompaniment. It is available on "Pawlo Humeniuk - King of the Ukrainian Fiddlers" (Folklyric 7025). Taking the key change into account, the two performances are very similar.

Humeniuk recorded this after emigrating to America. The title is half Ukrainian and half Jewish, translating roughly as *I'm Going Along Drunk*.

SZÓL A FIGEMADAR

The Figbird Is Singing was once a very popular melody in Eastern Europe. It was known in Yiddish as *Nokh A Bisl* (*A Little Bit More*) and became the basis of *Palestina* notated later in this chapter.

This version is played by the Orchestra of Tiszakorod on the 1991 album "Szatmari Bandak" (Hungaraton 18192). This is a gypsy group from the Szatmar region of Hungary, featuring two violins and a double bass. The tune is delivered with alternating light, airy tone and slashing, biting bowing. Their playing is also filled with bits of rhythmic rushing and dragging, lasting only a few notes at a time. Accurate notation of this effect is beyond me and would probably be impossible to read. It has got to be heard.

In measure 2 the second C♯ is given a "half" grace note, i.e. a D note is not completely depressed on the A string, resulting in a glottal-like "catch in the sounding of the C♯.

"OREA POUNE TIN ARGHI" EXCERPTS

Old styles of Greek music have had a strong Oriental flavor possibly stretching back to its Classic Age. The centuries of close contact with Turkey kept that vein strong while Western sounds were also assimilated. There was a large Jewish population in Greece proper until World War II and Greeks were the ruling functionaries in parts of Eastern Europe in the 19th century. The degree of musical interchange, if any, is not clear.

The next entry is from the island of Naxos. Much of the Greek Island folk music exhibits an exciting blend of the sensibilities of the East and West. A couple of tunes that I have heard in this style have Jewish themes. (See the liner notes for "Greek-Oriental Smyrnaic-Rebetic Songs and Dances" Folklyric 9033.)

This tune featured vocal with interludes of the violin of Yorgos Konitópoulos and *sandour* (a cymbalom-like instrument). During the vocals the latter two supply a rhythm of:

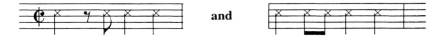

along with occasional eighth note runs. These figures are the same as those played in "Freylakh from *Die Mame Is Gegangen in Mark Areyn, Opshpiel Far Die Mekhatonim* and *Tsiganeshti* found earlier in this book.

I have included violin bowing notation (i.e. the slurs indicate bow direction changes). There was no overt harmony on this recording so my chord notation is just a possible interpretation. Alternately you may treat the tonic note of each chord as the key of the scale of the moment.

Between each instrumental section there is a vocal on the recording which I have not notated. The last measure or two of each part is an entrance into the rhythmic accompaniment to the vocal, not part of the melody *per se*.

The A notes in parentheses in section 2 represent the pitch at the beginning of the indicated slide. That pitch has no duration. The same is true for the parenthetical C in section 4.

Section 4 is an approximation of the *taksim* portion of Konito'poulos's solo. (This is a rubato or semi-rubato exploration of the modes of a piece.) He played over the santour's steady motive notated above, but my division of the meter into four beats to the bar is misleading. The whole solo might be thought of as taking place in one long measure or a series constantly shifting meters. (Transcribers sometimes use dashed bar lines on rubato portions of tunes.)

The notes that endure for more than a measure actually involve several bow strokes, but are phrased completely legato. Perhaps significantly, the changes in bow direction frequently take place after about three beats with slight accents. For example, the first three measure of G♮ are bowed something like:

The pitch length and frequency of the slides in the taksim is also noteworthy. (Walter Zev Feldman informed me that this is <u>not</u> truly a taksim, but a rubato improvisation on the melody of the tune. A taksim is not based on the melody. It certainly sounds taksim-related to me.)

162

163

SEHNAZ LONGA

The Turkic people known as the Ottomans ruled parts of Eastern Europe for centuries, so some of the "Oriental" character of klezmer might have been introduced or reinforced by the music of what is today's Turkey.

The Erkose Ensemble performed the following piece on "Tzigane - The Gypsy Music of Turkey" (CMP 3010). The *longa* is a kind of dance. This group consists of clarinet, violin, kanun (a zither-like instrument) and hand drums. The first three play the melody more or less in unison, but with much variation of embellishments and timing. The drum often beats the same timing as the melody notes. There was no chordal accompaniment so my choices are merely one possible interpretation of a Western harmony. Ordinarily there is none in performance.

According to an article in Ethnomusicology by Walter Zev Feldman, klezmer versions of this type of dance were recorded by Josef Solinski under the titles *Rumeynisher Fantazi #1-4* in the early years of the Twentieth Century in Poland. (See "Bibliography" for the reference.)

The piece begins in the same scale as klezmer numbers like *Odessa Bulgar* (see "Freylakh" chapter), a minor scale with a sharp fourth degree of the scale. I am interpreting E to be the tonic. By the end of the first section the tonic seems to have modulated to A in a new scale.

The order of sections is 1-2-3-2-4-2. On the album the clarinet goes on to play a taksim following what I have notated. The key signature of sections 3 and 4 is G♯ and D♯! In section 1 is F♯ and D♯.

165

LITURGICAL MELODIES

These are tunes associated with the various synagogue services, be they prayers, blessings or readings from the bible. All were prayers first, with various melodies composed for the same prayer over time in culturally diverse communities. The ones that became part of the klezmer repertoire have been treated differently than secular tunes, and reserved for solemn occasions.

The sensibility of the liturgical melodies is one of the important sources of klezmer music. Both acknowledge a base of Eastern influence with accretions (sometimes overwhelming the former) of local genres.

ADON OLAM

This prayer, *Master of the World* usually closes *shabbos* services. It evinces no Eastern influence and is apparently of German derivation. This version is based on the kind of melody that might be heard in an American synagogue. A version of this tune can be found on Andy Statman and David Grisman's "Songs of Our Fathers" (Acoustic Disc 14).

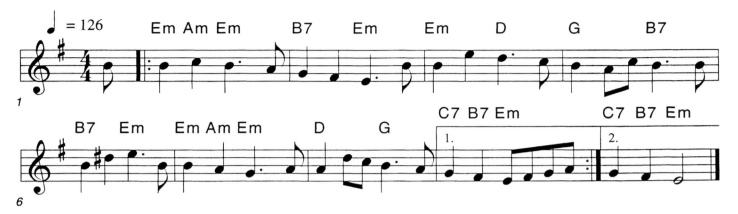

AWVEENU MALKAYNU

The melody for *Our Father, Our King"* is only used during New Year services, the most solemn observance in Judaism. It is based on vocal rendition and is only one of many melodies employed for this prayer. It uses the typical oriental-sounding major scale with b2 and b6 steps. (For example, see *Ma Yofus, Grichesher Tantz,* sections 9-11 of *Rusishe Sher #2(A)*, and many others in this book.)

Although not treated as such in a synagogue, the meter could be a hora. The chords are my own invention.

BAY ANAW RAWKHEETZ

This is a *shabbos* prayer in the Aramaic language, with the approximate meaning *We Desire*. This is the basic melody as sung in some synagogues. It is performed in a semi-rubato, freely rhythmic manner, with oratory-like pauses and fermatas.

The chords are my own invention.

B'ROSH HASHANAH

On the New Year is another vocal melody from the High Holy Days. I have omitted most of the mournful ornamentation a cantor usually supplies.

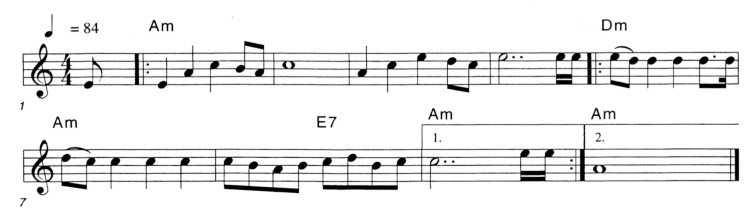

168

YISMEKHU V'MALKHUSKHO

They Shall Rejoice in Your Kingdom was learned from Leon Schwartz's violin rendition ("Like a Different World" Global Village 109). It is played very slowly with semi-rubato phrasing. I felt that cut time notation was much easier to read.

This prayer is said on the Jewish *shabbos*. The melody was used in the Yiddish song *Shpilzhe Mir a Lidele oyf Yiddish* (*Sing Me a Song in Yiddish*).

Schwartz sometimes phrases the first four notes of measure 7 as:

He varies his phrasing of series of eighth notes, as either straight eighths or sixteenth-dotted eighth-sixteenth-dotted eighth. Measures 12 and 14 are sometimes phrased:

169

DIE GRINEH KUZINE

The Greenhorn Cousin was composed during the heyday of the Yiddish theater in New York City. The American version was a continuation of the development of this art form in the nineteenth century performed by a European, urban, Jewish intelligentsia. My rendition is based on a vocal arrangement and, as such, has little embellishment. The minor mode and harmonization is not atypical for klezmer, but the authors have increased the Western influence.

The freylakh section is instrumental and played at a faster tempo than the vocal section.

This song relates the tale of the arrival of a new immigrant; fresh off the boat and deposited with relatives. The words as my mother remembers them translate loosely to:

> *"A cousin has come and she is as beautiful as gold,*
> *With cheeks red as pomegranates and feet made for dancing.*
>
> *She doesn't walk, she skips, she doesn't talk, she sings,*
> *That's how this greenhorn is, Long Live Columbus's Land!*
>
> *I met with my next door neighbor who has a milinery store,*
> *She found a job for my cousin, such luck in Columbus's land.*
>
> *A few years have passed and my cousin has become a wreck,*
> *Under her blue eyes now stretch black rings, a curse on Columbus's land!"*

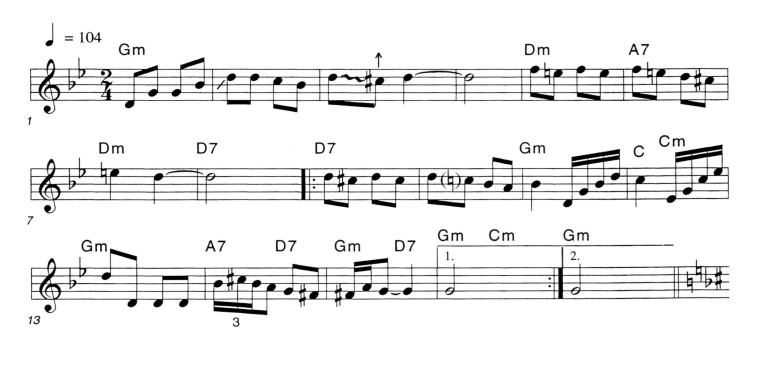
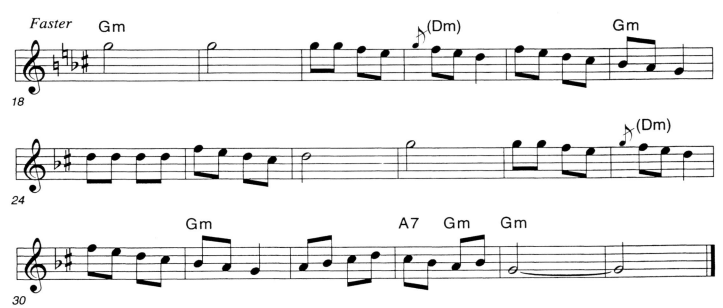

Yiddish lyrics by Hyman Prizant, music by Abe Schwartz
© Copyright 1922 by J. & J. Kammen Music Co.

PALESTINA

This curiosity was recorded by the Original Dixieland Jazz Band in 1920 in the hot style of the day. The melody was carried by saxophone with prehistoric dixieland jazz style accompaniment by other horns and drums. Sections 1 and 3 employ a typical klezmer minor scale, one with a ♭3, ♭7 and ♯4 steps. (For example see *Odessa Bulgar #1*, *Khupah Tanz #1*, *Mazel Tov Mekhotonim*, and several others in this book.) They also exhibit typical klezmer-like shifts of mode.

The third section is an Americanized version of *Szol A Figemadar*. (See this entry earlier in this chapter.) The last four measures are especially Westernized. As an interlude the band plays section 1 of *Ma Yofus* so it seems obvious that this was a genuine attempt at jazzing up a klezmer melody.

The lyrics have a deathless quality. It seems possible that at least some of these words were made up by children on the streets of the New York City in the early 1920's.

(to the melody of section 1)
In the Bronx of New York City, lives a girl who's very pretty,
Lena is her name,
Such a lovely girl is Lena, how she plays her concertina,
Really is a shame.

(to the melody of section 2)
She is a swell musician, she has a good position,
To go across the sea and entertain.
And now I know that Lena, is down in Palestina
and things are never going to be the same
They say that -

(to the melody of section 3)
Lena is the queen of Palestina,
Just because she plays her concertina.
She plays it day and night,
She plays with all her might,
She never gets it right,
But how they love her, want more of her,
I heard her play once or twice,
Oh murder, but she was nice.
They say that she was fat but she got leaner,
Playing on her concertina,
Way down Palestina way.

173

INTERVIEW WITH WALTER ZEV FELDMAN

I want the readers to be aware of an academic view of klezmer music. What is it about the music that is of scholarly interest? There is some promising research being done (a bit of which is cited in the Bibliography).

The evolution of this music is clouded by what is, for an American, a mind-boggling melange of ethnic identities shifting about with unknown degrees of cultural mingling in the relevant areas of Eastern Europe

An ethnomusicologist is trained to analyze music much more rigorously than philistines like myself. I found it best to ask a couple of questions and then let Doctor Feldman roll.

Besides klezmer, Doctor Feldman has researched classical and dervish music in Turkey. He currently teaches at the Department of Oriental Studies at the University of Pennsylvania.

I began with a request for something about the roots of klezmer.

Walter Zev Feldman (WZF): It seems that Bessarabia was the most important region when the klezmer genre was formed. [early 19th century]. Maybe that is a bit exaggerated. But it so happens that we don't have good documentation say, for the klezmer music of Lithuania or other regions. We know a lot more about the Ukraine and Bessarabia. For a variety of reasons having to do with immigration to America, we know more about what was played in those areas. It does seem that Bessarabia had a disproportionate influence, not just on the American version, but altogether.

Was there klezmer before Bessarabia? I am sure there was, and this tended to be preserved in the North, i.e. Byellarussia etc.

Stacy Phillips (SP): But was the earlier music "oriental" sounding?

WZF: Ahh, that's the question. There are kinds of tunes, if you look at just from the point of view of scales. If you go through [Moshe] Beregovski's book [see Bibliography], you find that most of the things called *freylakhs* are in *Ahava Raba* .[The scale that begins with a minor second followed by a minor third, in D: D-E♭-F♯-G-A-B♭-C-D. Tunes in this book that use this mode at least in part include, *Ma Yofus* and *Firn Die Mekhatonim Aheim*.] It is a common scale. Some people would use the word "mode".

If you compare the modulations, and the rhythmic breakup of the [melodies of the] tunes with other regional musics where the Jews lived; the Ukraine, Poland, Galicia, Byellarussia you find that these things are quite different. It points to a Near Eastern source, possibly Greek. For example, the dance music of most of the Ukraine and Galicia, the melodic rhythm tends to be symmetrical. A classic example would be [sings]:

You've got a kind of AB-BA back-to-back structure. [Feldman refers to the two 1/8's - four 1/16's melodic rhythm of the first two measures, followed by the reverse.]

You have various Jewish tunes like that, not quite like that, some are more elaborate and longer. A very old klezmer tune like [sings the first section of *Ma Yofus*, see page 112] You can see how the symmetry of the melodic rhythm works.

If you look at the klezmer tunes, especially in the Ahava Raba scale or mode, they tend not to be so symmetrical in that way. They're created on a different principle. They're not as regular. [sings]

There are internal syncopations and you don't have this [figure above] kind of back-to-back mirror image structure.

Even if they're quite short [sings a bit of the first section of *Rusishe Sher #1*]. They are created with this simple symmetry. Where do you find tunes of this sort? Well, they are unique. Anyone from the area would recognize these as Jewish tunes. It is not even typical of Romanian music. Probably, if you made a study of Greek *hasapikos* you would find similar patterns, but not very close. Although we know of a number of tunes that are considered to be hasapikos by the Greeks and freylakhs by the Jews which are equally typical to both genres. We don't really know but I tend to think that they were Greek first. Martin Schwartz of the University of California in Berkeley thinks that they were freylakhs first, which is possible because we know that in Bessarabia from the beginning of the 19th Century you had Ashkenazi Jews coming in large numbers. After Russia annexed it in 1812, you had the situation where Jews became very prominent in professional music. There were still many Greek musicians in Bessarabia and you had bands of mixed ethnicity. I wouldn't be surprised if much of this repertoire was created by these professional bands who played for Jews and non-Jews.

SP: Was the music of the Jews in that area Eastern or "oriental"-sounding before that?

WZF: Well if you look at the tunes in minor, then you often see a different structure altogether. A tune like:

The rhythmic structure is more symmetrical and European. But there is something between the rhythmic structure, melodic direction and cadential endings that is typical Ashkenaz. It wouldn't be mistaken for anything else. I don't think that the Greco-Romanian influence was important in creating those tunes.

Many of these tunes show connection to *nigun*. They were created primarily vocally. There you are dealing with Chassidism and their impetus to create these vocal dance tunes which began in the 18th Century. There you had a reason for creativity because it had a new function. The Chassidim didn't simply take existing secular klezmer tunes for their own purposes Not only that. They also created a lot of tunes.

This was mainly happening in the southern part of Jewish settlements. It began in the Ukraine. So some of the same influences which were operating on klezmer music also would have operated on Chassidic music. But at the same time there were more, you might say, standard Ashkenaz melodic principles that were also used to write Chassidic tunes.

SP: There was at least a predisposition towards Eastern sounding music from at least some of the liturgical music. Some of that must be very old.

WZF: Sure. The principle for the melodies of Ashkenaz prayers is a non-Western concept. It's an old concept. It's not even comparable to the principles in Gregorian chant. It seems that it goes back to First Millennium A.D. when the music of the synagogue and several Christian churches were being created. There were principles of relating melody with text which they all were working with at that time. My impression is that the concept of Ashkenazic chant goes back to that period. Of course, I don't think the actual melodic material of the chants goes back that far. Although it's many centuries old.

But it is an enigma. The actual notes that are used is certainly not connected with any one European group nor is it closely connected with anything in the Middle East.

SP: There are liturgical tunes like the one I used for *Awveenu Malkaynu* in this book which could almost be klezmer.

WZF: Tunes in triple time are one of the most intriguing questions about klezmer music. The most recent structures you have for these is the waltz on one hand and the *zhok* on the other. They are completely different things. You also have tunes that relate to various types of Polish dances which are in nigunim and klezmer. But we have a lot of these tunes which are not connected with dancing. Although zhok was sometimes just used as "street melodies" without tunes. Then there are tunes like *Awveenu Malkaynu* which are not meant for dancing. There are quite a number of tunes like the *Dobriden* ["Good Day"] tunes you can find in Beregovski. They didn't come to America very much. They were part of the traditional wedding that died out very quickly in America. Those have a particular relationship of melody to rhythm that show various influences, Polish, Tatar certainly, but *Awveenu Malkaynu* is not that either.

SP: Could you comment on the principles and patterns of modulation, both intra- and inter-sectional?

WZF: Joshua Horowitz has written a paper that he will publish at some point which goes through the modulations very practically. I don't know if it will be published in The States or Europe, but he's done good work analyzing the typical modulations. There certainly was a system. The repertoire that we have has very characteristic ones in the more elaborate three part tunes.

SP: In this book *Tsiganeshti* is especially filled with surprising changes.

WZF: [sings a bit of it] That is actually not klezmer music, it's Romanian Gypsy.

SP: But if a Romanian gypsy played it, you could tell that it wasn't a klezmer musician playing it.

WZF: I could imagine this played by a Gypsy orchestra with a slightly different rhythmic structure. I learned this tune from Dave Tarras. He said he learned it from [Joseph] Moskowitz. [See *Sadeger Khusid* and *Melodies From "Doina" Medley* #2 in the Freylakhs chapter.]

I don't see any part of it that really typical of klezmer music. The cadences are typically gypsy.

SP: I'm referring to the performance practices more than the basic melody...his phrasing and things I can't notate.

WZF: Tarras' style of playing is a Jewish style, but the notes he plays in *Tsiganeshti* are not. [sings second section of the tune] That cadence is typically Romanian Gypsy. The modulation [into section 3] is not typical klezmer.

There were separate Gypsy styles for Bucharest, Iasi, Argesh in Wallachia. People who know Romanian Gypsy music will recognize characteristic phrases from each of those places. Moskowitz was from Galati in southern Moldavia.

It's a complicated business because on the one hand, much of the klezmer repertoire comes from a certain kind of Romanian repertoire. But there were other kinds of Romanian music that never entered klezmer. There were things that got into the repertoire and dropped out and left only traces. I think a tune like *Tsiganeshti* represents a very recent phase of Romanian Gypsy music, recent meaning turn of the 20th Century.

We have some documents of the earlier stages of Romanian urban music from the early 19th Century. In them you see an earlier stage of the combination of Turkish *maqam* melodies and Greek folk melodies with Western harmony principles. [*maqam* refers to a way of dealing with modes vaguely akin to Indian ragas.]

SP: That's another question I had. When do you think harmony was introduced into this music?

WZF: It started in the 1820's-'30's. You had a very complicated musical life in those Romanian cities. There were still references to the *tambour*, the dominant Turkish city instrument [a member of the lute family]. There were Greek tambour players in Iasi, Bucharest and so forth. The pianos show up in Bucharest in the 1820's.

SP: So the introduction of the piano signaled the beginning of the use of Western harmonies.

WZF: No doubt. We have documents of what the Greeks listened to, and at that time they were still using the Turkish maqam system, purely. In the 1830's there is a collection from Iasi and by this time there is a mixture of elements though in an earlier form. Later that century the Romanians no longer played maqams in a "pure" way. They kept elements of maqams. They began to modulate quite freely without paying attention to the theory of Turkish music. They introduced chords where they thought them appropriate. We don't know exactly how this took place.

SP: Perhaps almost unconsciously, without an "art attitude" towards the music...just what sounded good.

WZF: There was a different aesthetics developing. A knowledge of some kind of Western harmony was coming in and had some prestige. Meanwhile the Turkish repertoire wasn't as widespread as in Turkey proper. Some places where the Turks ruled, their music had a deep impact, like Greece. Other places the effect was much more superficial. In Bosnia for example, despite the fact that much of the population is Muslim, the Turkish musical influence seems to have ended very early, though the Turks were there until 1878. Romanian music is much more Turkish than Bosnian music is. In Romania the ruling group were Greeks from Istanbul, and they brought Turkish styles with them. They also brought elements of Greek popular music from Istanbul and elsewhere.

SP: So I gather that most of the music in this book, recorded in America before 1930, is music that was developed in the late 19th Century.

WZF: The pieces that were anonymous, played by the orchestras in New York, Abe Schwartz, Harry Kandel - nobody owned those tunes. They were already established. Everyone knew the tune, and in some cases they were anonymous before World War I. They are certainly no younger than the 1880's. Someone like Schwartz was an adult when he came to America. He was musically trained in Europe. So he must have learned a repertoire that was considered standard by 1880.

So a lot of the tunes are no newer than the 1880's, a lot are considerably older - 1850's perhaps.

SP: From before the last layer of "Romania-ization".

WZF: Certainly. The last layer is recognizable. First of all it's the *bulgar* which is a specific Bessarabian dance. [See Feldman's article in Bibliography.] Zhok is also quite recent. [Joachim] Stutschewski is of Ukrainian origin and in his book [see Bibliography] he writes about zhok as if it were a new innovation that was not really Jewish. He left Kiev in the Ukraine in the 1920's perhaps. In Kiev in the 1920's, zhok was not yet klezmer music. It was Romanian or Bessarabian.

SP: As opposed to New York at the same time.

WZF: In New York the repertoire became Bessarabian faster. Jews came there from everywhere. Not everyone was a Bessarabian of course, but those genres became established as standards.

SP: How did the klezmer musicians refer to the tunes? How did they let other musicians know what they wanted to play?

WZF: I have no idea.

SP: Were the tunes that were recorded in the 1920's as medleys always connected with each other?

WZF: I doubt it. There was no substance connecting them. *Shers* were always played as medleys. They're usually two part tunes, not elaborate. Modulation was achieved by playing a bunch of different shers.

Tarras was no help to me with titles. He said that he didn't know what to call these tunes. He'd just make things up, and so did Naftule [Brandwine]. Rarely does the name make some sense. Abe Schwartz and Elenkrieg had all these fanciful titles, *Tate Siser* and *Oy Tate S'iz Gut*.

The only thing that was clear in those days was that a bulgar was a bulgar. In our generation people have no idea what a bulgar is, but then it was clear. Then there were shers, although there are plenty of freylakhs that could be shers. But the things recorded as shers were usually done as medleys. The zhok was something quite different of course.

There were many names for the freylakh, which was the most important Jewish dance. In Hungary they called them *khussidls* or *husit*. That word was used for two very different things. It could be used for something identical to freylakhs. But there are other tunes called khussidls which I think originate in vocal music. Some of this music is purely instrumental and some is ambivalent. It could be used as vocal music. The most instrumental of all the music is the bulgar. It does not relate to any vocal genre. It goes back to dance music. It is derived from the *sirba*, but the sirba doesn't seem to have caught on in Jewish music. There are a few recordings and transcriptions, but evidently it was not popular in New York at that time.

Bulgar has a totally different principle of relation rhythm to notes than vocal music. Tarras' style is well suited to bulgar because he likes lots of note changes, which bulgars give you a chance to do. Vocal music is not for that. It's relatively difficult to sing a relatively large number of notes in a short time with a quick tempo. Jewish dance music singing was a much different thing with fewer notes.

The *honga* was another Moldavian dance. It's not related to the freylakhs or bulgar. There are very few examples of it in the Jewish repertoire.

Hora is a general term in Romania with different regions having different meanings. The more general meaning is a binary rhythmic form [like 2/4] at a moderate tempo. In western Moldavia the term also can refer to the zhok form. In the East, in Bessarabia they use the term "zhok".

SP: Are the dances that people are doing today to this music historically accurate?

WZF: The only teacher I know is Michael Alpert. He's done some real research into it.

SP: There hasn't been an obvious continuous tradition? He's had to try and piece these things together again?

WZF: Yes. There are several reasons for that. My generation was brought up with Israeli dance, coinciding with the creation of the state of Israel. And because of the Holocaust many people didn't want to do dances from the *shtetls*. So there was a gap. The people who knew the European dances were pretty old.

My father danced when I was a kid. Someone ten years older than me in some cases saw freylakhs and shers. But you have to remember that Jews had a different approach to dancing. It was not an exhibition of one person but the creation of a certain ambience in a group. Yiddish dancing tended to be less extroverted than other folk dancing of Eastern Europe. It was not as formal as Western European folk dancing, though the sher does have kind of square dancing elements. There is a feeling in it that it took me a long time to appreciate. When I was younger I was impressed by Romanian and Greek dancing. Some of those dances were done by Jews, like the bulgar and the Ukranian *kolomeyke*.

Partly because it was not very spectacular Jewish dances tended to be ignored in America. On the one hand it was very collective, it addressed the collective of the people, not the individual. The dancing that was individual - there were arm movements that were very expressive and unusual.

It's a question of what kind of situations people felt they could dance in a more individually expressive style. There is an enigma here that is not fully understood. Where did the expressive style exist in secular contexts? The Chassidim used it in some of their contexts, but it's not clear about where it existed secularly.

There has been a continuum of cultural expression from religious to secular, but in America the religious element became increasingly marginalized. Things that were related to the purely religious in Judaism were things for Shabbos and holidays only. There was a split that didn't exist in Eastern Europe.

It's mysterious how this happened, but somehow the audiences and musicians understood that certain kinds of musical feeling was too close to religious expression and they weren't living the kind of life in which that type of expression was appropriate.

SP: Given the New York klezmer sound, is there an Israeli klezmer style?

WZF: Sure.

SP: Is it completely different sounding? Does it sound Romanian?

WZF: I have heard recordings of the Sefad *Meron* repertoire, the indigenous Israeli klezmer.
In Israel you had the old Ashkenaz settlements, mainly in Jerusalem and Sfat. In Jerusalem they were extremely orthodox; they didn't allow instrumental music so there were no klezmorim there. In Sfat there was a custom of a yearly pilgrimage to the tomb of Shimon bar Yokhai, so there had to be instrumental music for that. I think that weddings were also celebrated with instrumental music there.

As far as I know some of these people may have come from klezmer lineage but often not. [In Europe families tended to pass on the music profession.] Yakov Mazur is writing about this in Israel so he may have some information.

SP: Do they play the same repertoire?

WZF: The Palestinian Ashkenazic musicians copied the same repertoire that we had in New York from the recordings. So you will hear a number of Dave Tarras and Naftule Brandwine tunes. If you go before that, there was a repertoire mainly of freylakhs which sound very much like the minor scale freylakhs, not the *Ahava Raba*, that we know from Eastern Europe. On the other hand, their performance style is rather different. The basis of their style needs to be analyzed. One problem with them is that they aren't professional musicians. Many are not from lineages of klezmer.

They didn't practice very much so it's hard to know whether they mean to be playing what they're playing. Their understanding of rhythm is sometimes deficient; they always have drumming, and the connection between percussion and the melody is not very well coordinated. It's clear that they've adopted certain cliché's from Arabic drumming and sometimes they try to make the melody fit. It's not an ancient feature. They might play [on the drum]:

This influences the phrasing of the melody. And there seems to be a tension often with the melody trying to preserve the phrasing of European klezmer and the percussion has its effect on this. I've come to find it interesting but I don't think they've yet created their own synthesis.

I am not clear as to what repertoire they have between the older minor key freylakhs and the newer Tarras/Brandwine repertoire from the '20's and '30's.

SP: On a different subject, where does what is commonly considered Israeli music come from?

WZF: I'm not the man to ask. There is some scholarship going on in Israel recently.

Israeli music went through several distinct phases. I never studied it but I heard quite a bit when I was younger. In the earliest phase from the first *Aliyah* [immigration] in the late 19th Century many people tried to imitate Arab music. There was this sort of simplified Arab music.

At the same time and also in the next phase there were a sort of Russian proletariat songs with socialist content and Russian folk tunes that a lot of the settlers knew. That was a very big element. To some extent they interacted but the Russian and Arab derived music were separate things.

There is certainly a Chassidic element in Israeli music partly because much of it had a very optimistic character, which was appropriate to the mood at the time. All this was before there were many composers in the styles.

I should add that the [Israeli] hora seems to be derived from the bulgar.

SP: How about the background of the clarinet style. Does it follow the same path as the music?

WZF: The clarinet was not a characteristic Romanian instrument. The violin was used much more. It's quite recent in Greece as well, except in Epirus where it is a good deal older. I don't think that had direct influence on what the Jews did.

This music was predominantly a violin music. There certainly was a lot of contact the Jewish and Romanian Gypsy violin styles. Jews learned from that very sophisticated style and related to it. That's before the clarinet arrived.

SP: The clarinet eventually dominated the music. Where does that style come from?

WZF: We only have a few examples of European recordings of klezmer clarinet players. The clarinet in Europe almost always played behind the violin even though it's a louder instrument, but there were famous clarinetists by the end of the 19th Century.

Its hard to think that the kind of virtuoso clarinet playing we know in American klezmer could have developed in Europe. Greek playing is not the same - their way of slurring. Greek-American clarinet - some of those people listened to Jewish clarinetists. I think it had a definite influence on Greek-American clarinet, more than the reverse.

SP: So that laughing and chirping stuff is an American klezmer style.

WZF: Yes, I suppose so. Also the use of the lower octave seems to have originated with Dave Tarras.

SP: So Brandwine might have been part of the first generation of clarinet virtuosos.

WZF: No, probably the second generation. Earlier than that we hear of flute virtuosos, playing the wood baroque flute but not clarinet. There was no single Jewish clarinet style; [Naftule] Brandtwein and Tarras had very different styles, whereas Jewish violin seems very unified in Russia, Poland, Romania, etc.

[I then played a bit of the recordings of three pieces from the "Related Genres" chapter and asked for comments on their relation, if any, to klezmer. First up was *Birladeanca*. Having demonstrated my ignorance of the region where klezmer was nurtured, Doctor Feldman kindly explained some its geography and history.]

WZF: Birlad is a town on the western side of Moldavia, west of the Prut [River that now borders Romania and Bessarabia, that is, "Moldova".. I think Dragoi is from around there.

This kind of tune is not very closely related to klezmer. I've heard a lot of tunes like this from southwestern Moldavia. Its melodic construction is not typical of any kind of Jewish music.

SP: Was there a sizable Jewish presence in this area?

WZF: Yes, but the area of real musical symbiosis was not there but in Bessarabia. However much of the Romanian repertoire there is in klezmer came form West Moldavia.

SP: There was a Moldavian influence on the development of klezmer.

WZF: Yes, but this is not the Moldavia I talked about. There are three separate zones called Moldavia [which are also called Moldova]. They are all significant but in somewhat different ways.

Bessarabia is between the Prut and the Dnestr River. It became part of Moldavia in the 15th Century. People there were predominantly Tatars and Slavs. The Turks conquered Wallachia [now the southern part of Romania] in the middle of the 15th Century. In the early 16th Century the Moldavian princes made an agreement with the Turks to be a vassal state.

Western Moldavia is mostly highlands, mountains and foothills; the East is mostly lowlands. There were few Jews in the highlands. The Turks made it easier for the Jews to settle. Remember there weren't many Romanians in Bessarabia. There were mostly Tatars and Ukranian and Russian Slavs. The Turks built a number of fortresses in places like Khotin and Bendery., and where they built them Jews could settle easily. Originally they were probably from Crimea, Turkish or Tatar speaking Jews, not Ashkenazi.

In the 17th Century you have Ashkenazi coming down from Galicia and the Ukraine but the Moldavians didn't want Jews and Muslims settling all over the place. They were able to limit the settlements.

In the late 18th Century the Austrians took the northern part of Turkish Moldavia called Bucovina [now in Ukraine and Romania] and attached it to Galicia [which they had expropriated from Poland. Are you following this?] There already was a significant Galician Jewish presence there. In 1812 the Russians annexed Bessarabia. The Bessarabia bands were often both Jewish and Gypsy, and the repertoire often had characteristics of both musics, as well as of Greek music.

[I then played a bit of *Orea Poune Tin Arghi*.]
SP: There is a Greek influence on klezmer.

WZF: Of course.

SP: Are the same West Asian influences heard in this recording as in klezmer?

WZF: Not exactly. This is Greek Island music. It's a very sophisticated relationship between voice, rhythm, instrumental interludes, and the improvisations. I don't know the history of how this style developed. The Jews never developed a comparable style. This is more relevant to certain types of Romanian Gypsy singing with instrumental accompaniment. For Romanians this was tavern music played by professional Gypsy ensembles.

SP: This is a kind of music that someone unfamiliar with vast number of music styles of Eastern Europe might make a connection...it has that "semi-oriental" feel that puts it in the same bag as Romanian Gypsy, klezmer, some Turkish...

WZF: The basic genre is something other than klezmer. It's a dance tune with an integration of singing, dance phrases and non-metrical improvisation. It's danceable, but I think it's primarily meant for listening. Yiddish music didn't develop this genre. The types of Romanian music you can compare this to were not the things that developed into klezmer music. The melody does not relate to any type that's well known in Yiddish music.
He is not playing a true taksim.

SP: He is playing rubato though.

WZF: Yes, but a taksim is something else. A taksim is not based on the melody. This is a variant of the melody. This musician could probably play a taksim, but this is not it.
In Jewish music the term taksim had been used before doina came in. It is not clear what they meant by that.

SP: Not necessarily what is meant in Arabic music.

WZF: Certainly not. There was a kind of melody that Romanian Gypsies played in accompanying ballads which they called taksim, and those things are very much like doinas, but not quite. They have certain kinds of melodic phrases that are not typical of doina. No doubt that influenced what the Jews considered taksim; it is possible that some Turkish influence entered through the Romanian taksim however.

There are a few of these rather mysterious recordings, like the one that Abe Schwartz did where he changes the tuning.

SP: The double string playing. [In this tuning the A and D strings of the violin are switched and another notch is placed in the bridge close to the E string. The E is tuned down to D so that octaves can easily be played. The bottom two strings are tuned to A, an octave apart. I have heard the Schwartz recording and a cut on "Greek-Oriental Songs and Dances" (Folklyric 9033) called *Tsifte-Teli* that employ this technique.]

WZF: Schwartz's recording may be a taksim. It's certainly not a doina. *Tsifte-teli* means "two strings". In Turkish music it's a general term for Gypsy dancing. The origin may have to do with the tuning of the *kamenche.* [a West Asian spike fiddle] Leon Schwartz also had a tune like that.

It's clear that before the middle of the 19th Century klezmer music had many more of these Greco-Turkish features. Some of the melodic ideas that we now have in Greek and Turkish music were certainly in Yiddish music. They've left some traces.

So something like this tune, I can't say it never had anything to do with Jewish music. I'm sure it had something to do with the music of 150 years ago. But after that time other things became dominant.

[I then played an excerpt from *Sehnaz Longa.*]

WZF: This is extremely relevant. *Longas* are Turkish tunes that imitate Romanian Gypsy music. Turkish music was an imperial music, so different elements of folklore evolved with it in different countries in the empire. In different periods Bulgarian dancing, Greek, Romanian were fashionable in Istanbul. In the early 19th century Greek *sirtos* were popular. In the late 19th Century Romanian derived music called longas were popular. Jews picked up on these. There are klezmer tunes that can be traced to these, mixed with hasapikos, a Greek urban dance.

New York City, May 25, 1995

INTERVIEW WITH ANDY STATMAN

Andy Statman is a major figure (perhaps <u>the</u>) in the current interest in klezmer. He achieved fame as a master of the mandolin in several genres before being drawn to the pre-20th century sound of clarinet. In our salad days Andy and I were members of Breakfast Special for a couple of years.

He currently leads the Andy Statman Orchestra, recording with same and under his own name as a mandolin soloist. Here is the viewpoint of not only a working musician, but someone who has deeply studied the music from that angle and as a member of the orthodox Jewish community. He might change your concept of what klezmer music is.

Stacy Phillips (SP): There is a lot of music being described as klezmer today that's not really klezmer. Could you talk about what makes an authentic performance?

Andy Statman (AS): The first thing is that klezmer is an instrumental form. Yiddish folk songs and theater music are certainly influenced by klezmer music but they are not klezmer. Klezmer is certainly influenced in turn by vocal music but the *klezmorim* were by and large professional instrumentalists.

There is a definite style with certain melodic structures but the overwhelming thing is the emotional content of the tune and being able to bring that out. There is a definite way which this is done. Just as you could play anything in a jazz style, you could play anything in a klezmer style, but it usually doesn't make for good jazz or klezmer.

So besides the melodic content and the underlying emotion there is the interpretation. As they say, that's what separates the men from the boys. It has to do with understanding the correct tone for the music on whatever instrument you are playing. Then it has very much to do with phrasing, ornamentation and understanding variation. . . particularly phrasing. The tone and phrasing is of crucial importance. Otherwise, like Irish musicians say, "It's not going to have the *craic*[pronounced like "crack", meaning, roughly *the right feel*]".

SP: When klezmer musicians got together, let's say at a wedding, how did people know what songs to play when the tunes had no names?

AS: I don't really know. The leader might say "Freylakh in D" or "D freygish" [a particular mode] and everyone would follow. Usually when you're working a lot in a wedding band you establish a certain order of tunes and the musicians eventually expect that order.

SP: When you're playing at a Chassidic wedding these days are you playing klezmer or what you might call Chassidic music?

AS: Chassidic music is a whole other ball of wax. A good body of what we call klezmer music is Chassidic. . . traditional Chassidic music played klezmer style. What's being played now at Chassidic weddings can be a whole other discussion.

Klezmer music is made up of a variety of primarily Jewish styles or non-Jewish styles that were made into Jewish styles. A big Jewish style source was Chassidic music. The hotbed of klezmer music was also the hotbed of Chassidism. Most of the great klezmorim came from Chassidic families. Dave Tarras and Naftule Brandwein for example.

SP: But is it true that there is a big opus of Chassidic music that has nothing to do with klezmer?

AS: That's not true. The point to make is that all Jewish music is basically a form of worship. It's all spiritual music. Klezmer is part and parcel of this. There is a whole ritual of making a bride and groom rejoice at a wedding. It's a *mitzvah* [roughly meaning *a good deed*] to do that. You have stories back in the time of the talmud where the great sages were dancing and juggling to help the bride and groom rejoice. The wedding is the holiest day in the lives of the bride and groom. The older musicians, until a few generations ago, had the intention of fulfilling this mitzvah of making the bride and groom happy at the wedding. The same goes for the dancers. So the music was serving a mitzvah function. These dance tunes are just one element of a much deeper type of Jewish music. In Chassidic music you have different melodies for different holidays. . . very profound stuff. It's a way of achieving a spiritual state and closeness with God and your own soul It's not just a dance form. It goes back to the time of the Temple when prophetic states were induced with the help of instrumental music. The rituals were all accompanied with music. Music is way of worshipping that goes back to the beginning of Judaism. This is ultimately where the music is coming from. . . particularly the body of Eastern European *Ashkenazic* music. The flavor that it has, even the secular music like Yiddish theater music, is still coming from this religious background. So it is able to evoke these feelings even though it's "secular". Even if it's a love song the music transcends that. Ultimately it makes people feel Jewish and feel joy in being Jewish. You're shaking hands with your own soul.

So in answer to your original question, klezmer is a definite style. It's not a hodgepodge. Many people make it out to be Jewish jazz and a secularized dance form. That's not what it's meant to be. It's an intent and a way of feeling and expressing music. As in any folk form when you get too far afield it becomes something else. It's fragile and you lose it. You can say it about bluegrass music, about Albanian music. There are Albanian bands playing a sort of rock and roll. Particularly when you change the rhythmic and harmonic underpinnings of a traditional music it begins to destroy the subtlety of the expressiveness of what the music has to say. Something intrinsic is lost. Klezmer melodies are, at their base, built on rhythmic patterns. There is something like a *clave*. [This refers to the basic rhythm of the Cuban *son montuno* form, popularly called *salsa* or *mambo* in America. The part of the pattern that Andy refers to is:]

If the drummer doesn't understand how the melodies are built rhythmically the band will not be able to phrase correctly. You also need to understand how the modes work. If they reharmonize they might mess up the modes. The modes are based on the simplest of chord changes if any. I have reharmonized things but the beauty of this music lies is in the real old style, which is very free and open and expressive.

They talk about the best of the old klezmorim who just played *tish nigunim* [tunes for the table] which are these old Chassidic rubato tunes. The doina is just the tip of the iceberg of that type of music that once existed. These go back and forth between cantorial chant, Chassidic tunes and klezmer. Thank God we still have the dance forms of the music, but there are deeper forms from which the dances evolved. . . meditative explorations of modes. These were played particularly to achieve a spiritual state. The doina which is the shepherds melody. It's a parable. The Shepherd calling his sheep is God calling the Jews.

SP: A lot of that stuff had Romanian, Gypsy and Turkish influences.

AS: Yes, but the thing to note is that, while there were these influences, the music was given a Jewish intent and feeling, just as Jewish music influenced these other style in turn.

In this society the context of where this music is coming from is completely unavailable to the average person. The closest thing is what happens in some Chassidic communities on holidays or *shabbos* [Saturday]. This is when instrumental music is *not* being played. People sing. There are still Rabbis around writing tunes that sound 150 years old. I've seen young boys playing an electric keyboard with no chops whatsoever, and they played like Naftule Brandwine. They understand the context of the music. Just listening to old 78 [r.p.m. records] will take you only so far.

I know for myself, playing many Chassidic weddings, even though a lot of the music now is more of a pop form, when you play the old nigunim, even in a pop way, they know how to dance to the music. Seeing that helps you understand the music.

Klezmer as a style hasn't been taken seriously and has been stepped on a lot. Jews particularly are so starved for something Jewish will respond to it. As Henry Sapoznik would say, "anything that even evokes the feeling," will suffice. It's a deep form, but it's getting a bit of the short end of the stick.

SP: Are the other rubato, meditative styles that you mentioned still alive, or at least available on record?

AS: Not really. Mostly what you have on record are doinas and *kaleh besetzen* forms. [For an example of the latter see the chapter of "Khosidls, Terkeshes etc".] If you listen to the real old stuff you hear a bit. I found that some of this stuff is flourishing in the Chassidic community, but not public. It doesn't go on records. They're still being written. The next album I'll do will basically be this type of music.

SP: I know that you play many weddings for the whole Jewish community, not just Chassidim, and of course there are concerts. Are there any other klezmer jobs you get?

AS: Yes. There are some religious-oriented events I play, sometimes in a *shul* [synagogue] or at some meeting place. Nowadays when someone wants the klezmer sound I do studio work. [laughs]

SP: It has become one those "world music" genres, like cajun accordion or Bulgarian singing, of interest outside Jewish communities.

AS: It's great music so everyone can enjoy it but particularly a Jew will feel Jewish when he hears it. [laughter]

SP: Please talk a bit about your relationship with Dave Tarras.

AS: Well, basically I was Dave's protégé. I have three of his clarinets, he wrote music for me, and he wanted me to carry on for him. I did an apprenticeship with him, which was basically spending many, many hours with him. In the course of a visit he would take out his clarinet and he would play a little something for me. I might have a couple of questions and we'd listen to some music. A lot of what I learned was from watching him play, his body language, discussing music, occasionally asking pointed questions. I might play something for him and he would say don't do this or do that a particular way. Mainly it was through spending time with him that I learned.

He was from the Ukraine and descended from a family of klezmorim. On his last recording ("Music for the Traditional Jewish Wedding" - Balkan Arts Center US 1002) he had nothing to prove. Someone described it as sounding like an old black blues man from the Delta, just playing from his heart .

SP: He played some of the old sounds.

186

AS: Exactly. It's one of his best records. It's so expressive. I think he knew that it would be his last recording. I was very lucky to spend lots and lots of time with him.

I learned a tremendous amount from him though he didn't have a systematic way of teaching. I have been fortunate to study with a number of master ethnic musicians, and none had a method of teaching. I learned through osmosis.

I'm playing on an Albert system clarinet which is what the old klezmorim used. That has a different tonal quality than the Boehm system. [The latter is the current fingering system that became popular when keys were invented for wind instruments and replaced fingering holes.]

My style is equally, if not more so, influenced by Naftule Brandwine and Pericles Halkayas. Pericles is an old Epirot [Greek]/Albanian clarinetist who represented the old, traditional style. I studied with him for a long time.

SP: Anything else you'd like to say to the purchaser of this book about learning to play klezmer music?

AS: You should listen to the recordings made before 1927. Some of the playing was not great, some was brilliant, but they all have the feeling. Try to imitate them as closely as you can.

October 30, 1995 by phone from New York City

RECORDED MATERIAL

There has been an explosion in recording and re-issuing klezmer music. Many new ones are being distributed by European companies. Here is a list of sources for the music I used for the transcriptions in this book. You should check with some of the following for their current catalog.

a) Down Home Music (6921 Stockton Avenue, El Cerrito, CA 94530)
b) Elderly Instruments (P.O. Box 14210, Lansing, MI 48901)
c) Round Up Records (1 Camp Street, Somerville, MA 02140)
d) Original Music (418 Lasher Road, Tivoli, NY 12583)
This last firm is particularly notable for its access to foreign labels and the material in the chapter on "Related Genres of Music".

Refer to the introductory remarks to the tunes for the names of specific albums used as references in this book. The addresses of the record companies cited in this book follow.
a) Folklyric (10341 San Pablo Avenue, El Cerrito , CA 94530)
b) Arhoolie (same as Folklyric)
c) Global Village Music (Box 2051, Cathedral Station, New York City, NY 10025)
d) Flying Fish (1304 W. Schubert, Chicago, IL 60614)
e) Shanachie (37 East Clinton Street, Newton NJ 07860)
f) Yazoo (same as Shanachie)
g) Ethnic (previously "Balkan") Arts Center (131 Varick Street, Room 907, New York City, NY 10013)
h) Rounder Records (One Camp Street, Cambridge, MA 02140)
i) Smithsonian Folkways, phone: (202) 287-3262
j) Hannibal (c/o Rykodisc, Pickering Wharf, Building C, Salem, MA 01970)
k) CMP Records (155 W 72 Street, #704. New York City, NY 10023)
l) The Klezmatics album is available through 174 W. 89th Street, #5A, New York City, NY 10024
m) Acoustic Disc (Box 4143, San Rafael, CA 94913)

THE WRITTEN WORD

1. Notes to many of the albums cited as sources in this book are authoritative and chock full of the kind of background information that increases the listener's appreciation of this music.

2. *Grove Dictionary of Music and Musicians* (1992. MacMillan Publishers Ltd., London) has extensive articles on Jewish music and Dave Tarras.

3. *The Compleat Klezmer* by Henry Sapoznik (Tara Publications, Cedarhurst, N.Y.) is an excellent companion to this volume. Of particular value, along with about 35 transcriptions, are its interesting introduction to the history and practice of klezmer music.

4. *Jewish Music - Its Historical Development* by Abraham Idelsohn (Dover Publication, New York) is a dated but still very useful overview of Jewish music in general. Other researchers frequently refer to this text. However, Idelsohn mentions klezmer only in passing.

5. "Bulgărească/Bulgarish/Bulgar: The Transformation of a Klezmer Dance Genre" by W. Zev Feldman (*Ethnomusicology*, Winter 1994). This is a fine, concise and provocative discussion of the recent history of klezmer in America (up to the current revival) concentrating on the bulgar and hybrid bulgar-freylakh forms. It is currently available only in this scholarly journal.

6. *Old Jewish Folk music: The Collections and Writings of Moshe Beregovski*, by Moshe Beregovski and Marc Slobin, (University of Pennsylvania, Philadelphia, PA) A translation of some of the work of a pre-World War II Russian researcher, with many music examples. The Russian version of this book contains more music. Until recently it was thought that the KGB had destroyed Beregovski's recordings of the music in this book. However, this most important non-commercial collection has recently been located in Russia. The aural state of the cylinder recordings is still to be determined. Scholarly work is being done on the collection as I edit this manuscript.

7. *Ha-Klezmorim* by Joachim Stutschewski (Tel Aviv: Bialik) An, as yet, untranslated study of klezmer music in Hebrew, with many music examples.

8. *European Recordings of Jewish Instrumental Music, 1911-1914* by Jeffrey Wollock (ARSC Journal, Spring 1997) - a discography of about 200 sides, mostly Russian, many of which have not yet been located. The journal is put out by the Association of Recorded Sound Collections.

Two organizations that are specially good sources of information about this music are -

YIVO Institute for Jewish Research (1048 Fifth Avenue, New York, NY 10028) has recordings, books and pictures of klezmer musicians, as well as all other aspects of Jewish culture.

Living Traditions (430 W. 14th Street, Room 514, New York City, NY 10014) sponsors *KlezKamps* in New York and California where, among many other topics, klezmer repertoire is taught.

ABOUT THE AUTHOR

Stacy Phillips plays the violin and acoustic steel guitar (Dobro®). He has written 20 books on various aspects of these instruments. Stacy was a featured performer on the 1994 Grammy winning *Great Dobro® Sessions* (Sugar Hill Records). He currently performs with the Stacy Phillips Duet.